The Habit of Loving

Barbara Lazear Ascher

THE
HABIT
OF
LOVING

RANDOM HOUSE
NEW YORK

Most of the material in this work first appeared in substantially different form and under different titles in *Newsday Magazine*, and *The New York Times*.

Grateful acknowledgment is made to the following for permission to reprint previously published material:

CPP/BELWIN, INC., and INTERNATIONAL MUSIC PUBLICATIONS: Excerpt from the lyrics to "I'm Sitting On Top Of The World" by Ray Henderson, Samuel M. Lewis and Joseph Young. Copyright 1925 (renewed 1953) Leo Feist, Inc. Assigned to SBK Catalogue Partnership. All rights in the U.S. and Canada controlled and administered by SBK Feist Catalogue Inc. All other rights controlled by International Music Publications. International copyright secured. Made in the U.S.A. All rights reserved.

ELLE MAGAZINE: "On Compassion" and "On Trust" by Barbara Lazear Ascher. Reprinted from March 1988/April 1988 *Elle*. Copyright 1988 Elle Publishing. All rights reserved.

ALFRED A. KNOPF, INC.: Excerpt from "Depression Before Spring" by Wallace Stevens from *The Collected Poems of Wallace Stevens*. Copyright 1923 and renewed 1951 by Wallace Stevens.

Use of the title of "Frogs Eat Butterflies. Snakes Eat Frogs. Hogs Eat Snakes. Men Eat Hogs" by Wallace Stevens. Used by permission of Alfred A. Knopf, Inc.

NEW DIRECTIONS PUBLISHING CORPORATION and CARCANET PRESS LIMITED: Ten lines from "Danse Russe" by William Carlos Williams from *William Carlos Williams: Collected Poems Vol. I., 1909–1939*. Copyright 1938 by New Directions Publishing Corporation. Reprinted by permission of New Directions Publishing Corporation and Carcanet Press Limited.

Ten lines from "Asphodel That Greeny Flower" by William Carlos Williams from *William Carlos Williams: Collected Poems Vol. II, 1939–1962*. Copyright © 1962 by William Carlos Williams. Reprinted by permission of New Directions Publishing Corporation.

Library of Congress Cataloging-in-Publication Data
Ascher, Barbara Lazear.
The habit of loving / by Barbara Lazear Ascher.
p. cm. ISBN 0-394-56515-0
1. Middle-aged women–United States–Psychology. 2. Life change events–United States. I. Title
HQ1059.5.U5A83 1989 305.24′4–dc20 89-42790

Manufactured in the United States of America
9 8 7 6 5 4 3 2
First Edition

Book design by J.K. Lambert

FOR BOB AND REBECCA

It was the love of love,
   the love that swallows up all else,
    a grateful love,
a love of nature, of people,
  animals,
    a love engendering
gentleness and goodness
  that moved me
    and that *I saw in you.*

WILLIAM CARLOS WILLIAMS

*The habit of love cuts through
confusion and stumbles or contrives its
way out of difficulty, it remembers the
way even when it forgets, for a
dumbfounded moment, its reason
for being.*

EUDORA WELTY
The Eye of the Story

Contents

PAYING HEED

LOOKING BACK

Introduction

. . . .

I have a friend whose only tool on an archeological dig along the Dead Sea was a number-eight pure bristle paintbrush. "We were digging for the foundations of an ancient civilization, but we weren't allowed to dig," she tells me. "We were only allowed to gently brush away the sand lest we destroy what we might find buried there." For weeks my friend sat beneath a scorching desert sun, sifting sand until she uncovered columns that had supported a temple.

As I enter middle age I feel that I too am in the desert,

brushing away sand in search of my own foundations. Delicately, so as not to destroy that which I might find there. Delicately, so as not to destroy that which holds me. Unlike raucous, earlier years of building up and taking down and building up again with the devil-may-care enthusiasm of children at the beach, these are painstaking times. What we hope to uncover are ourselves.

If old age is a time of summing up, then middle age is a time of taking stock. A time of paying heed to matters of the heart, to the consequences of our loving and passions. It is a time of looking back at what we were, out at the world around us and into ourselves and those closest to us to determine what really matters. To discard what does not. I have come to wonder whether this is not some natural order that facilitates a more full-spirited, less heavily burdened journey to the end.

It's a time of knowing love well enough to learn its ultimate lesson: that life is a bit of a cheat. That with love there is never enough time. That without it, there is not time at all.

The Habit of Loving

The Life You Live
May Be Your Own

....

"When I turned forty, I stopped being desperate," a friend tells me. Earlier this week, another had said, "When I awakened on my fiftieth birthday, I was quite depressed, and then I said to myself, 'This is your life. It's not going to be radically different than it is now, there aren't going to be any big changes, you're not going to become a different person, so make of it what you will.' And somehow, I was able to accept that."

Acceptance of who we are may be the gift of middle age.

It seems to come with the realization, gained through steady and ofttimes treacherous experience, that we do not control the universe. My once desperate friend puts it this way, "I thought if I didn't accomplish certain things, acquire certain things, become certain things by the time I was forty . . ." She's unable to recall the imagined consequence, but it was probably along the lines of the world coming to an end. All she knows is that she's been released from the compulsion to become more than she is, and has settled down to the business of being who she is in fact. She's found that confrontation with her limitations has freed rather than condemned. It's odd how we go out into the world to prove ourselves before we know ourselves, and then once we know ourselves there's nothing to prove.

I am still new to the peace of such acceptance. Some days are more desperate than others. But then, I did not approach this phase of my life with willing grace. I was dragged kicking and screaming across the threshold. At forty, I still harbored the comforting conceit that I, like General Haig, was in control here. Even though a spinal injury had sent me to bed for the better part of that year, I protested to my physician, "I don't understand. I've always thought of my body as a twelve-year-old's body. I've always thought it was capable of anything." What I was really saying was, I don't understand, I thought I was immortal. God knows, I didn't want to forfeit that illusion of ultimate control. But circumstance left no choice. My body was out of control. There was nothing to do but to accept that fact, then to accept that I was not a neurosurgeon and to entrust myself to one who was, to allow myself to be saved. The fact that I was physically helpless forced me to confront a deeper helplessness and achieve a more profound and focused sense of responsibility. I was not invulnerable and I had to take care. From profound despair and fear came a certain acceptance of the limits of who I was, and rather than being disdainful, I became my own, more thoughtful guardian.

Although my experience was physically dramatic, I don't think it was all that different from the emotional ordeal suffered by my friends who speak of having come through the normal turmoil of early life to arrive at a later peace.

I think when my friend awakened on her fiftieth birthday she had reached a point where she could begin, in Montaigne's words, "to know how to enjoy our being rightfully," because she was ready to accept herself rightfully.

When I asked a friend who won a Pulitzer Prize when he was twenty-six, "What would you have done if you hadn't won?" He said, "Killed myself." I know what he means. At that age, the desperation is for achievement as the world measures achievement, in terms of titles, prizes, and promotions. One lives one's life as though its ultimate purpose was an obituary in *The New York Times*. Will there be anything to say about me? It is later that we begin to live for ourselves. It is in the middle years that we come to know that the life we live may be our own.

Not too long ago, when I was in my thirties, I was a traveller. If I couldn't hit the road every two months, a terrible restlessness set in. I was convinced that I had no choice but to satisfy my wanderlust, often leaving a bewildered and annoyed family behind. No Penelope and Telemachus they. It was a bitter and exhausting fight for the freedom to pack my bags and leave. It separated me from more than domestic shores; I was putting distance between myself and a legacy of women who had stayed at home. It seemed very important, as it is at that time in one's life, that I not be like those who came before. That I become distinctly who I was. Now, it's been a long time since my passport's been stamped. The journey has become internal. Perhaps that's where it belonged in the first place.

Even if we never leave home, life demands that we master the art of letting go. Letting go of our mothers' hands, then our daughters', and then our tenacious grip on cherished illusions of our own power and how life ought to be. It allows us a firmer grasp of life as it is, a kindlier embrace of ourselves as we are. In mid-life we're left with all that was ever ours to hold in the first place.

LETTING
GO

Adolescence

....

It's hot here under the spotlight of judgment. Sometimes I confuse my teenage daughter with the KGB or the Doges. Is this home or the Star Chamber?

I instantly take to heart my daughter's observation that I am a flawed specimen of my sex and species. Having been raised in the properly guilt-provoking Protestant faith, I'm the first to agree with her faultfinding. Somehow, in spite of all my efforts, perfection has remained elusive. Nonetheless, her complaints catch me off guard. It seems that chief among my faults is my facial expression.

"Don't make that face! You know how much it annoys me." My hand traces the outline of my jaw, my fingers search the frown lines of my brow, my tongue runs along the inside of my cheeks. Sensing no contortion, I respond, "It's a little hard not to make a face when one doesn't know one is making a face. This is my face."

The expression on hers tells me that's the point. This is my face and after seventeen years, it annoys her to look at it.

She resents my "immature appearance" yet accuses me of being jealous of her youth. This illustrates one of the marvelous achievements of adolescence, a symptom of this particular form of ambulatory psychosis. Adolescents are so certain of their own moral superiority that they presume that adults must envy their wisdom, energy, wit, and integrity.

Well, sure they have energy—they sleep all day, and as we, the household adults, turn in for the night after a hard day's work, they're ready to go out. As they exit, their hair moussed and sprayed to stiff perfection, they bemoan the lack of excitement and vitality in their parents' lives.

As to their wisdom, I remember it well. I'm not sure what has replaced *The Prophet* as this generation's tract for living. Perhaps the words of rock songs mainlined into their ears via the Walkman. Don't believe it when they tell you the purpose of the headset is better sound. The purpose is to keep adults out and the received knowledge in. When, and only when, they decide that you are worthy of hearing the profundities of Yellowman, Wham!, and Tears for Fears will the music be shared.

Theirs is the wisdom found in quotes under high school yearbook photographs. Things like, "I cried because I had no shoes until I met the man who had no feet." One of the current favorites is a catchy phrase from the movie *Flashdance,* "When you give up your dream you die."

I try not to laugh. What was once considered humor is now seen as criticism, and to teenagers, there is no humor in criticism. Self-righteousness exists beneath their studied insouciance.

The effect of the teenage psyche on parents is similar to that of a rare tropical disease, evading diagnosis and invading the blood and neurological systems. As their words and judgments course through our veins, we grow weaker. The integrity of brain cells is under seige. A serum is prescribed: Attack the invaders with assurance that we are good people, worthy of their kindness. The parent-child relationship is suddenly topsy-turvy. "Are you dizzy when you stand up?" the physician asks. "Do you sometimes feel a tingling sensation in your limbs?" Yes, indeed. Here we are, otherwise sane adults trying to prove to our young that we deserve their love and respect. Wasn't that their job, only yesterday?

In the chaos, the roles reverse. Just as children internalize the teachings of their parents, so have I internalized the criticisms of my daughter. When I dress in the morning, it is her eye rather than my own that scrutinizes the reflection in the mirror. I ask myself, "Why are you wearing that scarf with that blouse?" I can't come up with an answer. I look at my feet and think, "No offense, but those are the least attractive shoes I've ever seen."

This morning's newspaper advises me, "Be there for the child, maintain some line of communication." Apparently, the expert quoted, Dr. Anne C. Petersen, professor of human development at Pennsylvania State University, hasn't heard the news that the wires have been cut. We're on an ice floe with no post office, no pony express, no pens, paper, stamps, sticks, parchment, stones, or natural dyes.

Does Dr. Petersen understand what it means to "Be there for your child"? What it means is:

Be there so he can't speak to you
Be there so he can ask for money
Be there so he can think you're stupid
Be there so he will have someone to whom
 to feel superior
Be there so that there's an object for his disdain

A parent might wonder, why be there at all? Why not leave them alone to act that out with the household pets or a stranger passing through town?

A breakthrough! After two weeks of silence, my daughter asks me a question. So thrilled am I to be thrown a "line of communication," that I rush to "maintain."

"Mom," she asks, "if you could be anything other than who you are, what would it be?"

In my excitement over the spoken word, I answer from the uncensored bottom of my heart, "A lion!" I blurt out, "Except for the killing part. I don't want to snap the necks of antelopes. But the rest is great. You get to live in Africa, be graceful, beautiful, at home on the earth, proud, self-sufficient and . . ." A chill of silence falls over the African plains.

"Mom, I meant like Isabella Rosellini."

"Oh," say I. Shaken but determined to follow the advice to "maintain," I take a deep breath and continue, "Well, in that case, Katharine Hepburn. She was true to her sense of self and she dressed for comfort no matter what the prevailing style."

"You have to be beautiful to get away with that," she says, taking in my sweatshirt and blue jeans with one heavenward roll of her eyes.

Over and over I take the bait and run. On my answering machine the other day was her plaintive voice. "It's been a horrible day. Can we go out for lunch?" Sympathy is something I'm good at. Mothers rush in where wise men never go. So when she comes home, I put my arm around her shoulders. She shrugs it off and leans forward, leaving my limb suspended in air. I persevere, "So, what was so bad about today?" "I don't want to talk about it." I recall the advice of a friend whose son is now in his benign twenties: "The hardest thing to do," said she, "is to learn to keep your trap shut."

She's right. If it's peace you want, it's a lesson worth learning. To that end, never: (1) ask questions, (2) express opinions, or (3) react spontaneously. You'll have to be vigilant, as it takes time for those existing outside a vegetative state to master nonresponse.

A letter from a friend arrives in the mail: "We would like to invite your daughter to make her debut at the Junior League Ball. . . . It is a small, private, family affair. Our daughters thought it was the best night of their lives."

"Isn't that nice?" I murmur and then add, "I think that would really be fun." Vitriol and slamming doors.

"Stop trying to live through me. Just because you would like it doesn't mean I would."

AUTONOMY! is written across the banner they fly. Autonomy—with you in complete agreement and standing by. Independence is the battle cry, but symbiosis is the conflicting desire. Only this time you are required to bend, flex, and contort to their contours.

Just try. If you say you like their music or agree that it makes perfect sense to disco till dawn on school nights, they'll emerge briefly from muteness to state, "You want to live my life."

Dr. Petersen notes that teenagers' silent surliness is due in part to changes going on in their bodies that they do not understand. Changes are going on in *my* body that I do not understand. Why don't my knees support me, as they once did, for a full day of skiing? Why can't I dance until dawn? My orthopedist tells me there is a ruptured disc in my spine. He does not tell me the cause. But my daughter's pediatrician does. "Age," he says.

Another physician is consulted.

He takes out his pen and asks, "Children?"

"Yes."

"Boy?"

"Girl."

He draws the appropriate symbol on the chart.

"Age?"

He adds the number below the symbol and next to it writes, "Stress." He looks up, smiles, and speaks of hypnosis, painkillers, tranquilizers and his own experience as a parent. "If your children don't rebel, they're not the kind of children you'd want anyway. It all works out. When they're sixty or so they begin to realize you weren't as stupid as they thought." That's reassuring. I'll be eighty-two and, given the "natural atrophy of the brain that begins to occur after sixty," according to a neurologist friend, I might have become just as stupid as she thought.

I am tempted to do exactly what the experts in the article warn against: to drift into the quiet peace of open-armed regression, to fall silent, to give the world what the reporter refers to as "the adolescent cold shoulder," to give "one-word answers to . . . questions," to "glare in response to comments on dress or decorum," to close my "doors . . . against prying . . . eyes."

But no, Dr. Petersen warns, don't act "like an adolescent with your adolescent. . . . Don't think, 'Well . . . my child isn't talking to me, so forget it, I won't talk to him.' " Why not? This isn't a dinner party.

I would suggest to Dr. Petersen that there is another way. I suggest that adolescent behavior be met with adolescent behavior. That madness be met with madness, and lies with lies. When the child appears at the parent's bedside explaining, "I am three hours past my curfew because the car broke down," the parent should roll over and say, "Well, it really doesn't matter to me, because you see, I have more important things on my mind. I just got a call from the Coast. They want me to come out for a screen test first thing in the morning because a famous director saw me in the supermarket and could not get over my face, my body, my *je ne sais quoi.* He tracked me down through the address on the check I wrote for the groceries. It took weeks, but he searched relentlessly for me, his ideal of womanhood, Hollywood's next queen of the silver screen. So you see, I must get my beauty rest. Adieu, my dear, and goodnight."

Transition

··

It's April. The tulips have bloomed, the letters have come. Money has changed hands. It's a deal. My daughter has been accepted by the college of her choice. A signed contract says she's leaving home.

By day, she wears a T-shirt bearing the insignia of her destination. By night, she goes naked into dreams. Two nights ago she dreamed that we, her family, were together in a runaway elevator. As we plunged to our deaths we grabbed for each other's hands and repeated over and over, "I love you. I love you."

Last night I dreamed that I rescued my three-year-old niece from an oncoming truck. Plucked her from disaster with arms wrapped and fastened about her. A straitjacket fashioned to save her from without and from within.

These chimeras of the night hover about our breakfast table giving voice to our silent laments. One morning we fancy they sing lines from Walt Whitman's "Memories": "How sweet the silent backward tracings!/The wanderings as in dreams—the meditation of old times . . ." Simpler old times of early childhood and mothering when love and touch were foils to separation, danger, and death.

If these violent dreams had met midair, her runaway elevator, my runaway truck, phantasms unleashed by a letter of acceptance, the resulting explosion would have burst an orange hole in the night-blackened sky. By morning the fallout would have drifted over our home and into our hearts, making them unsafe for habitation. Don't eat the vegetables. Don't drink the milk. Don't feast on each other's eyes where the volatile energy of love is stored.

We avoid each other's glances and affect drowsiness as we share carefully edited dreams. Knowing that the realm of the unconscious is charged and ready for blast-off, we come to the table in protective layers—emotional space suits. Our words are muffled by radiation-resistant masks, and our hooded heads are snapped in place at neck and shoulder, lest we lose them. We could be the environmental control people, called in with boots, suits, and Geiger counters to proclaim Three Mile Island safe for the resumption of daily life. We suspected, back then, that they lied.

We suspect now that we do, as we chatter cheerfully of comforters and matching curtains to brighten a dorm room. The truth is that after August 30, the date of departure, there will be no resumption of daily life as we've known it. No more dreams will float through the room adjoining mine; a stranger's dreams will inhabit the room adjoining hers.

The ease of casual contact will give way to carefully plotted expeditions. Clear the calendar to come for the weekend. The foliage is great, come on up. There's three feet of fresh powder, pack your skis. You really should see this place in spring. Come now while the cherry trees are in bloom.

Perhaps we will become reacquainted in the course of weekend visits, perhaps not. Perhaps we will reach for each other's hands, not to save our lives, but to reconnect the channels so that love can flow. Will I find her "something rich and strange?" Or will the sea change be at depths that I cannot fathom? We do not speak of it, she and I, except to say, "Last night, I had the saddest dream."

There are two life events for which no woman is prepared: giving birth and letting go. "It must be a conspiracy of women," I tell my sister. "Of course," she responds. "If the truth were known, there would be no children." She's right. In order to populate the earth with those we can love, to become grandparents, aunts, family members, to keep alive the one phenomenon universally perceived as miraculous, we keep our mouths shut.

Even the lips of my Lamaze teacher were sealed. She was one of the early pioneers who arrived on these shores to persuade "over-drugged" birthing Americans to join the writhing wombs of Europe in something called "natural" childbirth. Basically the idea was to stay in control and relax. With the eager zeal of converts we were blind to the oxymoronic.

"Should you," she advised, "upon entering the 'transition period,' sense that you are losing control, ask your husband to press some tennis balls into the small of your back." "Transition period." The language of the conspirators. In fact, when I did sense myself "losing control" and asked the nurse for the tennis balls, she burst out laughing.

No tennis balls. But as the waves of "transition" swept me from consciousness, bubbles floated over my bed, message-bearing bubbles, like sea born bottles bobbing by the raft of a shipwrecked sailor. I grabbed for them and deciphered the wet words. "Didn't anyone warn you?" "No one told you that your uterus would feel as though it had been snatched between the jaws of a pit bull?" No, no one had told me. Not until the messages floated by.

One bubble carried the likeness of Ethel Kennedy, a reminder that some survive repeated transitions. I thought about my brother-in-law who, following the instructions of the Lamaze teacher, said to my sister as she entered the transition phase, "Imagine that you are on a beach in the Caribbean." My sister, meeting truth contraction by contraction responded, "No, Dan. YOU are on a beach in the Caribbean. I'm in Hell."

No one ever told us. No one had said that we, reserved, well-behaved young women who, in the second trimester, imagined ourselves Bellini Madonnas, would tell the obstetrician as we entered the transition phase, "Forget the whole thing. There's been some terrible mistake." No mother, no grandmother, no friend had ever warned us that pain defeats purpose. We had not been forewarned that there comes a point when we would forget that we had come here to have a baby. And no one had ever said that when that wrinkled mass of flesh was dropped onto our bellies, we would look down and be shocked by the thought that we weren't "adult enough" for this responsibility.

From that moment on, it becomes not so much a matter of

being "adult" as being fast on the feet and firm with the grip. Teaching the hands to be quicker than the brain, to reach out, close down and hold on. To grab the few tufts of downy hair as the slippery body eludes your grasp during the first bath. Your knees go weak as you rescue and realize that, but for you, there would have been a drowning. A death. But for you.

For the next seventeen years your hands are trained to save, to plunge in and retrieve the floundering. Until one day, when you are holding on for dear life, their fingers pry yours open one by one.

It would seem that mine are permanently frozen into claws. I am reminded of my childhood Sunday school teacher whose curved, white fingers pointed out the pictures of saints as we named them. It was the fingers, not Theresa, John, Mark, or Paul, that held my eight-year-old attention. I found them beautiful, like question marks in flesh. I did not know that there was disease there. That there was pain.

When I was leaving for college, my mother didn't cry. We didn't speak of nightmares or heartache preceding departure. I left with a collection of Keats under my arm and a beige, Shetland pullover on my back. Transition objects to ease the passage. Pride kept my smile steady and her handkerchief in her handbag. I don't know what she did when she returned to the car, sensed the absence of a passenger and placed her purse on the empty seat. She has never told me and I have never asked. I have joined the age-old conspiracy of women who do not reveal that the pain of the heart in letting go is like the pain of the uterus in transition.

It makes no sense. How can it be that just as we've swum through the storms of adolescence, just as we collapse on the beach, panting survivors warming each other's hands, we are to be ripped apart?

I begin to make plans that would keep us together. "Let's go out for dinner and celebrate." "Let's invite our friends in who are graduates of your college." Plans that attempt to throw up a wall in the path of her passage. Plans that resemble the fifty-foot ice sheets that recent Arctic explorers described upon their victorious return home. "It was like shoveling snow twenty-four hours a day," one of their leaders remarked, about getting over those mountains of ice, cutting the trails, and urging the dogs to their destination at the top of the world. I too am trying to push my way towards my destination, and my daughter to hers. And yet I am also the one whose psyche melts and freezes and cracks and builds up those almost insurpassable frozen barriers.

When you are at the top of the world, the needle of your compass begins to spin. That's how you know where you are. Do we want to risk that? Do we want to let our arms spin like that, not stopping to grab hold, to stay put? Are we struggling ahead to get to this cold and friendless place where old landmarks, old ways of navigation are lost to us?

I've been humming a song from my childhood. It goes something like this: "I'm sitting on top of the world. Just rolling along . . . Just singing a song." A jaunty tune that makes sitting on top of the world seem like perching on a sunny stone wall on an August day. Not so, say our explorers. The top of the world is damned cold. Seventy degrees below zero. To survive you have to eat fatty meat pemmican. The dogs eat fresh walrus meat. One of the sled dogs on the recent expedition to the Pole died when his master was airlifted out after an injury. "We couldn't figure out why," an explorer said, puzzled by the dog's quiet, insistent demise. Of course not. You couldn't survive the ice if you had the kind of mind that figured out why.

Leave-taking

....

"All is forgiven, please come home." This was no anonymous beseeching in the newsprint of a "personals" column. This plea issued from my husband, abandoned earlier that day by our daughter, who left for her first year of college. He would forgive the sweaters and socks, he said, the shirts, books, and glasses of apple juice—some upright, some not—on her bedroom floor, the occasional slammed door and fury directed (misguided, of course) at her parents. He would forgive everything, if she would just come home.

On the languorous August day of departure, separation

anxiety was as contagious as a yawn. We, the parents, strained fear through a cloth of instruction, attempting to eliminate any remaining lumps in character. I'm not certain that I actually reminded her "A stitch in time saves nine" or that he insisted "I want to be able to bounce a quarter off this bed." But we might have.

For her, college suddenly loomed as Destination Danger. It is doubtful that the knees of the departing Columbus, Marco Polo, Balboa, or Cortés shook more violently. Would she dare sail beyond the threshold guardians, ancient monsters poised on the edge of the world? Would she dare sail beyond this modern mother, a sentinel on the precipice of growing independence? When she landed, would the natives be friendly or hostile?

From the front seat of our over-burdened station wagon I established my authority through reassurance, "Dear, I am certain your roommate is not a wombat." She wanted to know, "Did I really, of my own free will, choose a college in the country?" She contemplated this mystery and determined, "I must have been on drugs." How else to explain forsaking smog, the wandering hands of male subway riders, Bloomingdales's hedonistic delights?

The three of us giggled like children daring each other on to perilous deeds. To roll across railroad tracks ahead of a charging train. To leap from a bridge into the icy waters of a country swimming hole. "I dare you!" The truth is, none of us dared, but we knew that to halt the forward passage of this fledgling, our daughter, would be as heinous a crime as that of two men recently arrested on charges of shooting migratory birds mid-flight. "They weren't in it for the money," their lawyer insisted. Neither were we. We were in it for passion.

Perhaps a passion similar to theirs: to have and to hold a

rare and fleeting thing. Samuel LiBrandi, an agent for the Fish and Wildlife Service, whose raid revealed the 588 stilled wings, offered another motive: People like "hawks, owls, ducks, or other birds for the fireplace mantel." Stuffed and mounted, a pretty trophy honoring a superior hold on life. Who could resist?

Somehow, we did, and thus continued until it was time to open the car door and expel the one we longed to hold. She seemed to hover for a moment in forgiving space, and then was gone. The two of us retraced our path in silence, the only sound an occasional errant beetle crashing against the windshield with a fatal click.

Back home, her absence became a presence, leaping from familiar corners and causing us to gasp as we passed her room, her empty closets, a telephone pad not scribbled upon. My husband paced like Achilles on the shores of Troy, mourning the loss of his dear Patroclus and "all the actions he had seen to the end with him." My silence was finally broken as two words squeaked past the lump in my throat. "My heart." I pointed to it as if signaling for the Heimlich maneuver, but no one could embrace me from behind and expel the knot of sorrow.

"The saddest part," I managed to say, "is that from now on she'll be a visitor." The way she started out with us when birth was too astounding to accept. Just passing through, we thought of this infant. You have to live with miracle before it can be anything other than a flash of incongruity from which you hide your eyes. When miracle became mundane, we became a family.

Now she will come again as a stranger, with mannerisms I don't recall. A way of standing, of punctuating a sentence. The adolescent personality is as malleable as infant flesh. It will respond to the press of peers.

Will there come a time when I feel shy as she crosses the threshold she once crossed several times a day dropping books, backpack, and clothing in her path, a trail to retrace should she lose her way? Will I have to follow clues to her character?

In the meantime, I have begun to experience the freedom I had expected only for the departing, not for those left behind. When I dress in the morning, it's with a certain dash, a certain flair. I grow bold in the absence of the voice that said, "You're not really going to wear *that*?" I become daring with prints and plaids. Fearless when there is no one to declare, "They don't go." All systems are go. I have invested in, and actually wear on the streets of Manhattan, black, hightop sneakers.

When she returns for a visit will she attempt to capture and stuff me into the old mold as I head out the door with bouncy shoes on my feet and a Walkman on my head? No matter that it's Bach rather than Dire Straits: "It's the idea, Mom."

As for her father, I dared not ask, until recently, if his heart, where it had buckled, was meshing again. "Do you miss her a lot?" I asked as we enjoyed the peace of a candle-lit dinner uninterrupted by the appearance of one who had declared twenty minutes earlier, "I'm not eating with you, I've already had pizza, a milk shake, two doughnuts, a peanut butter sandwich, six chocolate chip cookies, grilled cheese . . . am I fat? Tell me the truth. Will you tell me the truth if I get fat? Will you come right out and say, 'You're fat'?" This night no one appeared with a plate and the promise, "I'm not really eating with you," proving her point by commiting only one buttock to the chair.

In response to my question, he lowered his fork and stared

out across the top of the candles' flame. "Only when I think of her." Satisfied, I reached for his hand in a gesture of shared victory. We had adjusted with grace. We were home free. The flames bent before his sigh, as he added, "And I think of her all the time."

Letting Go

....

We were a parade of parents marching as though our clothes
were made of fiberboard. Mothers' lips, freshly colored, and
fathers' lips thin, retracted by age, held smiles as shy as boys
and girls on either side of the threshold of a first date.

Parents' Day. First dates with our children at college.
They, our awkward guides in this new land, pulled ahead, out
of the old formation of child between mother and father.
Long ago it had been pleasing to occupy that space, to reach
up for the swinging hands of parents, to be swept off the

ground and swooped above earthly dangers—puddles and sidewalk cracks.

But now their arms pressed rigidly against their ribs, save for waves of hearty greetings to fellow students. "Hey, John! How ya doin'?" "Hiya Lydia, what's happening?" Neither John nor Lydia were introduced to parents who hung back and feigned interest in foliage. We were reminded of Parents' Day in first grade. "See, Ma, see all the kids I know? See, I'm safe, I'm safe without you."

But were the parents safe? Their stiff faces and fixed smiles were those of foreigners newly arrived and at the mercy of strangers.

The scene returns to me now, four months and four thousand miles away. I believe it is the chickens that have brought it all back.

We are in the tropics. We have come to sit upon a crescent beach that forms a cup to hold the azure sea. We are here to become like the beach, to fill ourselves to brimming with blues and greens. To hold a mindless brew. To be pressed flat between sky and water and not protest.

It's been a dry year on the island and a hen has migrated from the village to the greener, grub-rich grasses of this irrigated land. Here she has hatched a dozen eggs. The chicks, yellow, brown, white, and dappled, run and trip in their mother's path. She forges ahead, scratching the earth in exaggerated motions, teaching them how to survive. How to run for cover at the slightest sound. There are enemies here— hawks, cats, and a gardener with designs.

Thursday at six o'clock, when the January sun has set, high tea has been consumed and nothing is planned until dinner, a woman crouches over a bed of cactus below our deck. "Come here, little fella. Come here." She stands, circles to the other side and carefully reaches her hands between the thorns. The peeping sound reveals her evasive quarry. "I'm so worried," she says, spotting us, the bystanders. "This baby chick became separated from its mother and it's not even a week old."

"Where's the mother?"

"That's the trouble. I can't find her."

I volunteer for chicken patrol, put on my shoes and set out. On my way down a path curving through scarlet cordia, flamboyant and calabash trees, I meet a man holding, in the closed palm of his hand, a baby chick. Shy at having been caught at tenderness, he jokes, "Just a little game the management arranges to keep us from getting bored." I tell him about the chick in the cactus, and suggest that we all meet back there should I locate the hen.

By now, it is too dark to go by sight. I listen, pressing my ears against the border of thickets, against the dark air of the night, cocking my head as if I were a bird myself, hoping to pick up the sound of scratching, of moving earth, of clucks and responding peeps. Stubborn, persistent, but growing discouraged, I return to the others. They have been joined by another woman who helps them surround the chick in the cactus. From this distance it looks like a game of ring-around-the-rosy.

"I've got it!" the newcomer shouts in a Chicago accent. Her eyes grin behind large glasses as she lifts the chick and holds it for a moment against her heart, like a mother cradling an infant. You can tell the gesture has an old familiarity for her. Later, I discover that she has five grown children.

"Now what?" asks the man among us.

Chicago answers, "The gardener told me he thinks their nest is up there." She points to a garden thick with jasmine and hibiscus. "Perhaps that's where we ought to take them."

We set out like crusaders, the righteousness of our mission

cleansing the crime of intervention. "Good," says the man surveying the protective cover of branches and vines, "there's no room for the hawk to swoop in here." He and Chicago open their hands and the two chicks tumble together, bumping head against head. "Stay together, little guys," says Chicago. Walking away, we make pleasantries and a few jokes as we grow nervous about our interference in some possible, larger design.

The next morning we meet on the beach. "I saw the mother with some chicks this morning. I think I saw mine," says the man. "No," says Chicago, "yours was yellow and there's not a yellow one with the group. I counted only ten. That means ours are still lost."

I too had checked at six A.M. No peeps, no chicks. I regretted our interference, and remembered the birds I had attempted to save through the stubbornly optimistic springs of childhood. The matchboxes lined with cotton. Eyedroppers for feeders, spilling water into bulging eyes as often as evasive beaks. The end always the same: a gray-fleshed, featherless form silent on a bed of cotton.

Very young children, if raised in a kindly environment, are saviors. They know what it is to be helpless, and in the years before they turn to attacking what they fear, they attempt to save. They save by mimicking the earliest acts of love, and in return, expect to be loved. I remained certain, in the face of evidence and experience to the contrary, that my birds, tossed from nests, would grow feathers, fat, and wings. I would teach them to fly and they would be mine. I saw no contradiction in that.

But why are four middle-aged adults rounding up chickens as if their own lives depended on it? We abhor separation. I imagine that each of us, as we search the grounds, is remembering an earlier search for a mother lost on the playground, in a supermarket aisle, between clothing racks in a department store. Memories of loss too early for words and comprehension are the fossil fuels of our mission.

On the beach, later in the day, Chicago lowers her book as she sees me approach. "They took our chickens." She smiles at her own sadness so that the corners of her mouth appear to fight against each other.

"What do you mean?"

"The gardener says he has a brood hen at home. So he threw out a big net and caught the chicks. He says they shouldn't grow up here, because then they're impossible to catch."

"And some of them will grow up to be roosters. The guests won't like that," adds someone from a neighboring chair.

"So that's why I heard the mother crying," say I and immediately regret my choice of words. The sentimentality. The anthropomorphizing. But the hen had been making an unusual ruckus that afternoon. It is difficult not to interpret that sound.

"Yes. They left the hen behind. I asked the gardener if it would make any difference if I threw my body in front of his truck, and he said, 'No.'"

I stare out at the bay and remember October and Parents' Day at college. Another big net had been cast at the end of August, had closed about its prey and delivered it to higher education. Barely a month later, we were not ready for a reunion. We were still brooding. We didn't know how to pretend that it didn't matter that we'd been robbed.

I wonder if we had stolen off into the night, my three chicken saviors and I, if we had fashioned our own wide net and walked to the village, to the gardener's house and crept into his chicken pen and caught the foster fledglings and dropped them into a sack and crossed the hill and followed the road through palm and Jerusalem thorn, and found the hen and opened the bag to deliver her chicks, would they have rushed forth to their mother? She to them? Would there have been a jubilant flurry of feathers? Or would they have remained still, as we did, not daring to move at all?

Mothering and the
Monsters Under My Bed

· ·

She writes from college to say that when she was five, or was it six, and her father and I would return home from our winter vacation in the Caribbean, she would race to embrace us, as if to do so was to embrace the sun. "I thought that you brought it back with you." She describes how she sniffed it out from the folds of our clothes, the browned skin of our limbs.

She no longer believes that we are carriers of the sun. We alone cannot bring light and warmth into her life. To be near us is not to bask in a glow.

But there once was a time when, to her, we were all-powerful. I didn't know it then, and fear that I may have abused that power, as one does when believing oneself powerless. Was I gentle enough with that tender shoot? How often did I walk over it in a hurry to get to my own goals?

There is one such moment I know. And there must be hundreds more that I am blessed not to recall. How else would one sleep at night or face the day? We would be fugitives from the laws of love.

But that remembered moment lives with me as a two A.M. monster under my bed. It is at that hour of greatest vulnerability, when one is naked and unguarded in sleep that the monsters go on parade. That those things we would prefer to forget come to scratch the backs of our memories.

They approach, sliding along on slippery monster bellies, navigating blanket boxes and dust ruffles to appear on their stage, the canopy above my head. My eyes are closed, but I know they're there and they know the audience is captive, which is all they ask.

They take the human forms of my daughter, then seven and feverish with the flu, and her mother departing for law school. There I am, sneakers, blue jeans, an old sweater with a rip at the elbow. At my feet is a red backpack holding twenty pounds of books, *Contracts, The Law of Civil Procedure, Real Property, Criminal Law.* Also at my feet is my daughter. Flannel pajamas enclose her toes, legs, and arms, but fail to keep her safe. She clings to my ankles, her face is wet with tears and her brown curls fall into her eyes and around my shoes. Why won't I save her life? Why will I take such a risk? To leave when she begs me to stay.

"Mommy, please don't go."

"I have to. I can't miss my contracts class."

"Please!"

These were not the wails of protest I had heard in earlier years when it was time to leave the playground. These were cries of fear and despair.

I was scared too. I was suffering from law school psychosis. I was suffering from women's liberation psychosis. In my struggle for freedom, I was taking a prisoner of war. And now I wonder, at two A.M., what kind of liberation was that?

My contracts professor was a short, intense, balding man schooled in the ways of terrorism. The Socratic method was molded to create the weapon of his attack and upon your return after missing a class, you were his target. "Ascher!" The sound that made one gasp for air. "Yes?" "Stand up!" he commanded. The knees would barely support. "Now, tell us the facts of the case." The facts. The story was always the best part. But it didn't stop there. This wasn't a soap opera. "And what were the issues of the case and what was the holding?" No matter how hard you had studied, how much sleep you had sacrificed to the cause, there was no avoiding the look of disdain that greeted your answer, the sarcasm in his response, "You don't mean to say that you really believe that?"

Had I not been suffering from the mental disease that pervades law school and all in attendance there, I would have answered, "Yes, I really do believe that," and sat down. But this was not real life. Students must withstand the authorized cruelty of professors because it prepared them, they were told, "For when you're before a judge."

If we'd really stopped to consider their reasoning, we would have come to doubt the entire judicial system—overseen, as we were led to believe, by the moral equivalent of military generals of a junta regime.

But law students have little time to stop and consider, otherwise the steadying hand of reason would have put my backpack in the closet on that day that replays itself in the night. The arms of reason would have enclosed a frightened child rather than holding her at a distance.

She had the flu. Her tonsils were red hot. Her temperature was 101 degrees and I feared my professor. I feared for my future as dictated by my narrow interpretation of the women's movement.

I would enter a man's world. I would bear a briefcase and a controlled demeanor. Intellect rather than emotion would guide my way. I would frequent judges' chambers, law libraries, corporate boardrooms. I would, in other words, make a difference. Be important. Matter. Be independent. Be free. And so, I picked up my books and went to class. I heard her wails through the door as I awaited the elevator. I hear them now, twelve years later at two A.M.

It is a given that, barring some defect of character, we love our children and desire to protect them from harm, cold, hunger, emotional duress. And yet, with clear-eyed vision, we also make decisions that victimize them. I knew that my daughter would survive while I attended class eighty blocks from home, and I believed then that attending class was of utmost importance.

I was young and caught up in a movement. It was no tragedy, if you accept Isaac Bashevis Singer's definition that no children died of it. All that happened was that a cloud bank moved in between my daughter and the person she had perceived as the light and the way. I was not her savior. I was capable of inflicting pain. I taught her how it felt to be abandoned, and in doing so, taught her something about love: That no matter its depth and passions, self-interest can lead it temporarily astray.

I cannot tell you about her psyche, that invisible, vulnerable mass delivered into my safekeeping. Will fear of separation follow her all the days of her life? Will the possibility of being abandoned be packed in the baggage she'll call love? If a future lover should depart, will she fall to her knees, her hair and tears spilling about his feet? Will the wail of grief lift to his ears and the heavens to mingle with loss remembered? The cries of the betrayed. Where do they go after they escape throat and lips? Do they become flesh and take up residence under all the maternal beds of post-Freudian history?

"I would hug you and smell the sweet odor of the sun. I believed you carried it with you," she writes, remembering.

The Forgiveness
of Daughters

....

She's been looking at Mary Cassatt's paintings of mothers
and children, and says, "You know, when I look at those
children, I don't experience envy. I experience familiarity."

When I look at those same paintings, I experience yearn-
ing, a painful reach of the heart towards those moments when
one could comfort. Fleeting moments, unlike Cassatt's
which, captured in pigment, endure. Ours were interrupted
by phone calls, dinner preparations, a social life. In Cassatt's
paintings there are no bills to be paid, no meetings to attend.

The dog is not howling to go out. Cassatt painted remembered moments of childhood such as my daughter describes, moments which rise to the top of memory's well and shimmer there above the more mundane and painful facts of family life. Childless, she painted from the memory of being a daughter, which is why my own daughter and I view her work from different perspectives. I look, and see not the comfort I gave, but the comfort I wish I had given.

I do not see myself as a source of reassurance and protection from the pains of the world. After all, she's now bigger than I. More outspoken. Strong in body and soul. When we stand, I have to look up in order to meet her eye-to-eye.

And I know my own psychic history. I know the times I let her down, times that weakened trust, drew a disappointed and hurt child away from her mother. The times she made me angry enough to scream in a rage that never enters the world of Cassatt's pictures. When she was two and defiant and when her defiance became physical in the form of a swift kick to the shins, and I, stunned, wailed to my husband, "I'm not sure I like her anymore!"

I know of the two A.M. feeding when we were new to each other and my milk came so fast she would choke and throw up and cry, and I would try again, and fail—the milk squirting into her eyes, her nostrils, and finally down her throat, but with such force, she gasped for relief. We didn't have our rhythms yet. We were unfamiliar with our ability to comfort and be comforted. Both of us felt awash in the world. Alone, with our enemy, our beloved. One of those dark winter nights of pacing and feeding and burping and soothing, I stopped to look out over Manhattan for lit windows, for signs of others suffering alone in the night. Instead, I caught our own reflection and was shocked by my small size, by the fact that in my arms there was a human life for which I was totally responsible. I thought, I'm not ready for this. I thought of the responsibility that would last a lifetime, and burst into tears.

I know all this and yet she sees me, through the eyes of love, as a Cassatt mother. Through the heart of forgiveness, she speaks of my ability to make her feel that the world and she are all right. Children's forgiveness of their parents is a perfect forgiveness, forged out of love and lacking self-consciousness. Unlike adults, children's forgiveness comes from the generosity of their hearts, not from overbearing consciences shorn up by community mores or church sermons. The most our consciences do is demand that we say "I'm sorry," demand that we put on a good show of it. But it is the rare adult who does not, when hurt, bear a grudge and wish ill upon the perpetrators. Children's forgiveness is another matter, it is natural, full-spirited and complete. So complete that it is accompanied by amnesia for the hurtful event.

One day recently, as my daughter and I strolled in Central Park reminiscing about her New York childhood and rainy days spent at double feature Fred Astaire movies in the Village, she said, "I'm so glad that I didn't have a working mom." Her mind had taken a flying leap from the darkened movie theater to the present, skimming across the top of painful memories. She does not hear her ancient outcry, experience her loneliness, or sense of betrayal and abandonment. That blank in her memory is filled in by my own remembrance. Mother's memories are not as kind. I think of a night during my first year of law school when the family was gathered for dinner and her tears began to fill the carefully constructed well in the center of her mashed potatoes. "When I grow up," she choked, "I'm not going to betray my husband and daughter by going to law school."

I don't remind her. Not now. I would rather bask in this forgiveness, accept it as a balm. I hear the old refrains of the dangers of repression and am tempted, for a moment, to say, "But you did have a working mom." But I don't. I am silent as I am now as she tells me of the Cassatt paintings. As she tells me of love.

There is a place for nostalgia. It helps us to forgive. Her memories, incomplete and flawed, colored by wish as well as reality, make it possible for her to grant me absolution. I do not indulge in a confessional. I do not beg forgiveness. It's given without asking. Now, of course, the job is mine.

The Habit of Loving

....

She calls to say that there are "boxes and boxes of Hemingway material" in the Kennedy Library in Washington, D.C. She invites me to join her in the pursuit. "If we go," she suggests, "we might uncover something no one's uncovered before." She'd like to do this for her term paper. "And we can visit the Phillips Collection," she adds in order to entice.

I agree and attend to the details—overnight accommodations, train tickets, the clearing of the calendar. It's all arranged. The adventure is set. Somewhere, along the way, we have made our peace and made our lives. After the upheavals of her senior year in high school, that year of anticipatory grief; after her freshman year in college, the first year away from home, when home seemed the repository of absences and silence shrouded me; after her sophomore year, the year adjustment began, when new life filled the vacuum left by loss, we live again. New lives. New companionship.

We need each other less, which clears the way for less complicated camaraderie. When describing the joys of her junior year in college she is kind enough to say, "I wish you were here to share it with me." We both know I don't belong. She is safe in her sentiment because I will not, in spite of my own wishes, drive north and appear at her Dutch and Flemish art class with a shiny new notebook clutched in my hand.

For as long as I can remember, I have been an enthusiastic reader of survival stories. As I turn the pages, the world I inhabit gives way to a much less benign environment. I join the protagonists in mountain treks, across treacherous passages where snow swallows our limbs. My couch becomes a life raft low on supplies, as sixty-knot winds and thirty-foot waves threaten our lives. When we, the protagonists and I, emerge alive—when we are reunited with civilization, hot soup, warm sox, and dry underwear, when we are delivered into the arms of waiting loved ones—I am inspired for days by evidence of the outer bounds of the human spirit. These life-threatening adventures are for me the externalization of spirit-threatening upheaval.

Life's stages exact their toll. It is only in an unexamined life that one can move through change as if it were just another cocktail party. Change forces us to raise our arms in surrender, to open our fists and forfeit the old habits to which we cling. When my daughter left home, it was the absent exercise of habit, as well as the person, that I mourned. The habit of meeting after school. The habit of trips to libraries and museums. The habit of sharing daily life and caring for her well-being in the most mundane matters, from the early days of zipping snow suits to the later demands to be home by midnight.

Now the habits are broken. I no longer suffer a physical craving for her companionship. I am no longer overcome by jealousy when I pass her old school at dismissal time and witness the happy reunions of mothers and children. I no longer pine for those gentle times of compliant youth. The past has been surrendered. Letting go took three years.

There are methods for speeding up the process, but I don't think they offer a true cure. The kids can become so obnoxious before they leave home that the parents are counting the days until departure. The parents can overschedule their lives with careers and meetings and social engagements, assuming they won't even notice when their home is child-free. I believe the reason these methods fail is because the only relief from the pain of loss is through the pain of mourning. Following that tortuous path is like joining my adventurers on their journeys out of snow and ice, through the wilderness, across the sea to rescue. There are no footsteps, no sign posts, the journey is individual and our lives depend on it.

I have read the statistics. When you are widowed, you are advised not to make any decisions or change your life in any way for one year, the assumption being that it takes that long to get your wits about you. The psychic pain of divorce, they say, begins to subside after two years. I have never seen the statistics for the mourning period following one's child leaving home.

Perhaps there are no statistics. After all, such a study would hardly be grant-bait. We, the smooth-talking, fast-living adults of this world are expected to be above needing our children. It doesn't fit the idealized feminist format that a woman is perfectly capable of fulfilling herself by herself. Never mind that this is a state verging on the hydra syndrome. Needing one's children has been seen as crippling kids and parents alike. Need, endemic to love, has become confused with the Jewish-mother jokes, "You don't write. You don't call." Such comparisons miss the point, confusing insatiability and need.

Of course one needs one's children. It is not a natural human state to love selflessly in the sense of loving and not expecting love in return. Such love is saintly, not familial. In families, as we teach the young how to return love, we teach the first lesson in reasonable expectation.

We need our children to love us in return in order to know the quality of our own loving. It is our songs of love, and their resounding choruses that sing us out of isolation and into existence as a family. We need our children to remind us of the joys of spontaneity and playfulness. We need to be touched by their enthusiasm for discovery, to be reminded that life is a series of discoveries preceded by mystery and struggle, and accompanied by the thrill of new vision.

And so we'll go to Washington, my daughter and I, to search through dusty boxes, the repositories of another's mysteries and discoveries. To see what we can find, because, says she, we might find something nobody's ever found before.

In the National Gallery

··

She reaches for my hand as we stand before the Rembrandt. "I can't believe it's here!" she exclaims, and adds, "I think I might faint."

Except for the fact that it is nineteen years older, this hand feels familiar, retaining an old restlessness and a few childhood calluses. I don't dare move lest she ease her grip, just as, when she was an infant asleep in my arms I would barely breathe for fear of disturbing the complete contentment. As though breathless, I could create eternity.

Now, nineteen years later, I am satisfied if this is all the eternity there is. The return of simple gestures of love.

When she was four, we made regular excursions to the Metropolitan Museum. Then I would reach for her hand when words were not sufficient to express the wonders of Manet's black, Monet's blue, Vermeer's golden light. My hand would conduct the passion. My hand would ground us. Now, she returns the favor.

I have come to think that life is not necessarily one large circle, but rather many small ones, each with its closure, its moment of resolution.

And thus, as we stand in the National Gallery, I am content in a way that is infrequent but sufficient. It is one of those moments that inspires one to think, "This is what we are about. This is the joy towards which I was striving, though I didn't know it then." This is a journey completed.

I have a friend who says, "Life is not about being happy. Life is about problem solving." He's wrong. Such a life would be a long day of paying bills or figuring out the income tax. It fails to inspire. It only asks that we complete the tasks that demand completion. How could one get out of bed in the morning if all that lay ahead were problem solving? Even Einstein loved to play.

What gets us out of bed is the possibility of joy.

For my friend, life more nearly resembles chess than poetry. I could dismiss his premise on sexist grounds, claiming that men don't have time for play, for fun, for standing in front of paintings with their children's hands in their own. That the old grindstone and Rembrandt don't mix. But that's absurd. Joy is not a party favor given out at ladies' luncheons. Joy is what comes when you go out on a limb and hang there for a very long time. And the limb is not a single-sex club. All are invited to dare.

I cannot imagine having approached motherhood as a job limited to teaching problem solving. I saw it as the one job in life for which the central requirement was the ability to know, convey, and teach joy. It certainly was not solely about clean faces and hands, good table manners, hand/eye coordination and please and thank you and share and don't hit and don't bite and don't spit on your hostess's floor.

Among the happiest memories of early motherhood were regular visits to the grand old mansion between Park and Madison Avenues on Seventy-ninth Street that houses the New York Society Library. There we would sit on the floor, with our treasures from the stacks spread out around us: *Amos & Boris, The Runaway Bunny, Corduroy, Madeline.* There, as the power of the written word began to reveal itself, I was moved to say, "When you learn how to read, a universe will open up for you." And I saw the door to that universe open a crack when she looked at black letters against a white page and saw them as words. "The cat," said she. Joy abounding.

The door to her happiness opens wider. From William Steig to Catullus, Bemelmans to Rembrandt in one long, steady, and not unrelated leap.

Is it not just such possibilities for joy that keep the museums and libraries open and concert halls full? Surely, the audiences are not compelled to come in out of the cold in order to solve problems.

The caretaker of our park is a problem solver. He rakes the leaves and sweeps up discarded condoms, beer bottles, and cigarette butts. His glance is rarely higher than the rims of the trash cans he empties. But every once in a while he leans against his rake, folds his long, brown fingers over its handle and rests his chin there. He gazes at the East River, following the tides and the barges that buck or flow with it. He does this most often in the early morning hours of late March when the mockingbird has taken its accustomed perch in the thorn tree. "Two hundred and fifty of 'em," he tells me one day. "The mock has two hundred and fifty songs to sing." Those were the only words I've ever heard from this bent and silent man who works his way through trash towards a pension.

I would guess that it isn't the promise of pension and the challenge of problem solving that brings him out instead of calling in sick. It's the possibility that maybe he'll be there for song number two hundred fifty.

I often think of the moment in Truman Capote's *A Christmas Memory* when he, a young boy, and his best friend, an elderly woman, send their Christmas kites soaring against a milky December sky and she, looking up at the bright airborne colors, exclaims, "I could leave the world with today in my eyes."

I have felt the same way in moments of joy, knowing that each such moment is a closing of the circle, the successful completion of life's essential task.

Perhaps my friend would argue that climbing Mount Everest was problem solving. And flying solo across the Atlantic. And travelling across the Arctic by dog sled. Perhaps he would say, "Problem solving is essential to survival. And if it's joy you want, there is deep satisfaction when you have met the challenge of a particularly knotty problem." I suppose he could claim, "You can consider the importance of joy because you don't have to consider the importance of bread on your table," and he'd have a point. But I would disagree that it was problem solving that inspires our explorers, our adventurers, our scientists. That is not what makes one strap on the knapsack. Load the sled with dried beef jerky. Become expert in celestial navigation.

It is not what inspires one to set out on the greatest adventure of all, becoming a parent.

We don't do it to become heroes, although it is a heroic task. We do it because we know there's something left undone, that there is joy we haven't known and perhaps, even for a fleeting moment, we'll meet it, heart to heart.

For this moment, as we stand in front of Rembrandt, my daughter's hand in mine, it's quite enough, it's all the eternity I require.

TALKING
AGAINST
TIME

On Pain

....

I don't remember summer that year. And what became of winter and spring? Was it cold? Did it snow? Did the apple trees blossom and fill the air with heady perfume? I don't know, I can't recall.

"We'll pack her up like an egg," my husband declared, with shears and measuring tape in hand. He measured the roll of tufted, blue foam rubber. He measured the car. And then he measured the body that had turned against me, my own. That is my only memory of summer. Travelling through the countryside spread across blue foam, staring up at blue sky, a body sandwich.

A ruptured disc, damaged nerves, spinal neurosurgery. The simple facts of a nonfatal illness from which chances of recovery are excellent. They called to tell me the facts and the odds, but no one was home; I'd checked out months ago. Prolonged pain is like a fire in the house, it causes you to flee and wander homeless, slipperless, and in a nightgown. Your feet follow the line of streets, not your command. You are no longer in command. You stare into the eyes of strangers, or those who somehow seem familiar but are blurred by the persistent smoke that surrounds you. Why do you stare at them? You are looking for the person who will say, "You are not going to die."

"I think it has to do with the right side of the brain," a pragmatic friend told me when I attempted to describe the sense that too much pain for too long had lifted me from the here and now and dropped me onto another plane of consciousness. She was wrong. This was uncharted territory. I began to wonder about Flannery O'Connor, who lived within a body slowly wasted by a disease born on the whim of a single gene. Did a life of pain open the door for her rare insights into the state of grace? Did her writing come from that same state of grace? Where did she spend her life—the life of the mind? I suspect that her passion for peacocks had something to do with the fact that she wasn't really here at all, but had passed to some world in which the golden and blue fans of feathers were more harmonious than the red earth of her native Georgia.

Pain did not deliver me into O'Connor's "habit of being." I am without her soul, her devout and inspired faith. What I, and the patients with whom I shared a waiting room across the months, seemed to experience was a sense of "otherness." When called forth by the young physical therapists, each of us, in various stages of agony, would respond to the question, "How are you?" with the expected, "Fine thank you." Fine thank you, as we relied on hands, arms and the grace of gravity to elevate us from the curve of a chair. Fine thank you, our voices said, but our eyes were blank, sea surfaces without clouds, without reflection. There were others who responded, "*I'm* fine, but the leg's not so good."

A divorce from the self is one way to remain sane, amid pain. And there were other methods at work in that waiting room. None of us ever looked directly at the other. If someone glanced from foot to staring eye, both sets of eyes retreated quickly to the floor: fear of contagion through sight. None of us wanted to catch the other's misery.

There were those who talked, compelled to tell their tale. It didn't matter that no one listened. People in pain are like the wandering minstrels of the Renaissance—any occupied space becomes their court. If the story is told often enough, perhaps the demons will become manifest, made visible, and mastered through words. Made visible and inviting empathy.

They could talk forever, it wouldn't matter: Pain is immune to empathy. One can sense, sympathize, lay on hands and chicken soup. One can probe and palpate. But one will never know another's pain. It is as if snarling guard dogs, electric fences rigged to shock, and brick walls taller than a man have been erected at the heart's border. No one has ever succeeded, not our poets, composers, philosophers or physicians, in making a chink in the wall large enough for our hands to meet and conduct the current of empathy. One suffers pain alone.

Pain is suspect, as though one's character were defective.

I could hear it in my own language. My problem was that I had a "bad" back. Others in that waiting room had "bad" legs, "nasty" spasms. Few of us were going to die, in fact, but we felt that something was dying, and it was. We were losing a benevolence towards the self. We became tangled in the undergrowth of pain, where metaphor grows like weeds, where a ruptured disc becomes Jung's "shadow"; sciatica, Blake's Tyger in the night; the spine, Dante's underworld. Sometimes I think we stared at the floor because, like children caught in the act, we were ashamed of ourselves.

We all regressed together in that room, month after month. It was as though each of us was waiting for Mother to pick us up from school, but she never came. Our bravado, denial, and fear were those of abandoned children. One day, as I automatically filled in the blanks of yet another medical form, I was chagrined to discover that in the blank following "Mother's name," I had written: "Mom." We were all waiting for Mom.

We were waiting for love to rescue us, and should it fail, for ourselves to rescue love. During that period I read and reread William Carlos Williams's poem, "Asphodel, That Greeny Flower," and began to understand what it might be like to be old and facing death with the knowledge that one's loving was flawed. "Hear me out," the poet begs his wife of many years. "Listen while I talk on against time." We are, all of us, talking against time, but we don't know it until that uncharted part of the brain is tapped by anguish. And then we know that all loving is flawed. Is there time? Time to perfect it? In the waiting room, the hands of an elderly couple would meet atop a single cane and remain there locked together until the doctor called.

You cannot live with pain and remain unchanged. Like the

narrator of Robert Frost's "Wild Grapes" who claims a new
life after being rescued from the branches of a tree, who after
swinging "suspended with the grapes" becomes aware that
"the life I live now's an extra life." If you are fortunate
enough to touch ground after being suspended by pain, suspended for so long that you are tempted to ease your grip, you
will not return as the person you were before being lifted from
earthly delights.

Celestial Navigation

··

This man loves his stars. "Betelgeuse," he says, splitting the
darkness with a nobby finger, so white it appears to glow.
"That reddish star. She's in her dying phase, but she's good
for another few hundred thousand years."

Obedient and eager to find what we expect to be there, we
follow his finger, lifting up our heads to the heavens. We are
like the children in John Hollander's poem, "The Great
Bear," straining to decipher the "frosty, irregular polygons of
our own devising." But this is no child's play.

Four of us have gathered on a tropical beach in response to a handwritten sign taped to the desk in the hotel lobby. STARGAZERS! SEE TAURUS! THE PLEIADES! AURIGA! AND MUCH, MUCH MORE! IT'S TEN O'CLOCK, DO YOU KNOW WHERE YOUR DIPPERS ARE? SEE YOU THEN, TEN SHARP, REC ROOM, THEN TO BEACH FOR STARGAZING!

One of us has come with a mission. A man in his seventies, his body long and tremulous, breathes heavily, and glances about as nervously as one who has returned to the Church after a twenty-year lapse and is uncertain whether he faces salvation or damnation. Either possibility makes him anxious, and his agitation grows as he fails to find the constellations pointed out to him. He raises his hand and waves it like a third grader with the right answer. He calls out, "But what if I get lost? How do I find the North Star?" His pale skin and pink pate would not serve him well if he were cast adrift.

Our leader, a local sailor and star buff, attempts to soothe in the way he has learned to soothe himself when sailing alone at night, when, but for stars, there would be no difference between sea and sky. He points to what he sees. "There's the Big Dipper. Just follow the cup, it points right to the North Star." He smiles with satisfaction. Some things you can count on.

Not so, states the worried man. "What if I can't find the Big Dipper? What if it's below the horizon?"

"Ah, then you look for Cassiopeia. See there? The upside-down *M*?"

"No, I don't see it, I don't see it at all!" Does he fear Poseidon's wrath, should he feast his eyes on Cassiopeia's fair beauty? His voice has the edge of one experiencing an examination dream. "But I'm not prepared! I'm not prepared!"

He looks so safe, this vacationing stranger in the steady

company of a wife, portly and still but for startled eyes that dart about like sand fleas. The two of them had been sitting in a corner playing cards when our teacher opened the lecture with the question, "Are you stargazers?" It was the mention of the North Star that had caused the pale man to slap his king of clubs and three hearts on the table, stand up and join our group of four.

Like most inhabitants of a tropical resort in the dead of winter, conversation was immediate among those who had never met.

"How long have you been here?"

"We come down for two weeks at Christmas, and two now."

"How's the weather at Christmas?"

The dialogues are always the same: Where are you from and how long have you been here? Voices making connections as vague as webbed stars. Words with which to trace ourselves, as "frosty and irregular" as Hollander's constellations, precariously perched on the edge of a volcanic whim in the Caribbean Sea.

The nervous man says he's from Canada. He would have been more content to stay with kings and clubs, than to search for constellations. Safer at the card table than here on the beach, straining skyward and losing his balance. His anxiety is contagious—the stars begin to make us nervous. A middle-aged blonde woman, unable to spot the Pleiades, orients herself to earth with a quick look at trees and sand; she is moved to tell us that she's born witness in the past. "Once, when we were in California, I saw the most amazing thing. I saw the moon and Jupiter and . . . what was it . . . was it . . ." She massages her temples to ease the way for the memory lingering there.

"Mars?" asks the gentle teacher.

"Yes! That's it! The moon! Jupiter! And Mars! All lined up!"

"I saw it too," says he.

She's also seen Sagittarius in Saybrook.

Her teenage daughter keeps her eyes on the ground and searches for shells along the edge of a phosphorescent gleam. Unlike her mother, who has come for stars and knows better, she's out for earthly delights.

Our teacher tries to regain control of the group disintegrating in its intensity to see in the dark. "Orion is here every winter," he says. The surprise is that no one responds, "Me too." It's becoming clear that no one wants to submit to stars, to be passive before such a cold, indifferent light. But what about us, is the question we want answered. Enough about stars, what about us?

Cassiopeia is setting and the man from Canada had better look fast if he's to be saved tonight. I take out pen and pad to draw the constellation before it disappears behind a beckoning mountain. I want to find my way back tomorrow, to tell anyone who's willing to listen, "See over there? See the stars that look like an upside-down *M?* That's Cassiopeia." I might even tell them the tale of the goddess herself, who, in daring to proclaim her beauty, was condemned to hang upside down for eternity. A public hanging for the world to see. I might wave my hand to give the right answer, but what kind of answer is that? There is no moral here, in these tales of vanity and unremitting revenge. We give stars purpose as we give them form, and we are wrong to do so. They do not exist to show the way. Should you reach for them as you tumble in your forward motion, all you'll come up with is a handful of night air. At least the shell-collecting child has something to show for her nocturnal pursuits.

No. There are no answers here for the fearful man. For

days now, ever since his arrival, he and his wife have stolen down to the beach in the early morning, before other guests awake, to secure chairs for themselves in the same shady spot beneath sea grape trees. Even though the rules in our welcome book clearly state, "Please be considerate and do not save beach chairs," they pile two chairs high with towels, yesterday's paper and tubes of sun-block. Their stealth is marked by tracks in the sand similar to those left by a female turtle returning to the sea before sunrise after egg-laying.

The fearful man regularly arrives in the dining room fifteen minutes before meals in order to sit at the same table for breakfast, lunch, and dinner. As the sun rises, he and his wife come bearing flowers and place them in a water glass to form a centerpiece. "Now, you leave these here all day. Don't move them," she warns the waiters. Oleander, frangipani, bougainvilla, and poor-man's-orchid, this earthly booty stakes their claim, wilts at noon, and is dead by nightfall.

The Death of a Dog

....

In the days of the dog's dying a scent of decay suggested something drastic beyond our vision and beyond our help.

We remembered recent hurricane victims, open-mouthed and incredulous as they stared into space once filled with the tops of trees. They wanted to know, how could winds, weaker than predicted, fell a fifty-foot oak? The answer was that the roots had rotted and could not brace a tree against heavy weather. Rotted in the secret intimacy of deep soil while life above went on as usual. Nests were built, tire swings hung, and picnic tables set in the shade of boughs. Weakened roots could support these frivolities of spring and summer, but not the gales of autumn that hauled them heavenward where branches used to be.

We, who have lost a dog, are as shocked as those who lost maples, oaks, and pines. We shake our fists at fate and its stealth in snatching lives. We stamp our feet and speak of fairness, as if life were a child's game bound by rules determining wins, losses, and who gets to go first. As if facts were marbles, smooth-surfaced aggies controlled by the swiftness of a thumb. No fair! cry the cheated children. No fair that the dog grew old and sick, that bones took dominion over spirit and flesh.

We knew the dog was leaving when he turned his back to our approach. We wondered, is it pride, or the deep privacy of death that turns the dying from earthly love? But we weren't ready for abandonment and stubbornly followed the path of his retreat.

I don't share prehistoric man's spiritual partnership with beasts. My walls are not carved with images of horses and ibexes, and unlike tribal hunters, I don't look to animals to learn how to live. And yet there is a remnant of that ancient harmony as I face the death of a dog and find myself contemplating many deaths—real and imagined, past and anticipated. What would my reactions have been had I been widowed instead? Would I act as I do now, compulsively cleaning, determined to rout out death as if it were a dust ball? As I throw out leash, collar, tick shampoo, and drinking bowl I wonder, if my husband rather than the dog had died, and this bowl were his shoes, would I drop them into a garbage bag along with all other possessions no longer possessed?

A parade of ghosts follows in the wake of my broom. Grandparents, old friends, the boy I loved at sixteen who died before we learned how to still our pounding hearts. I entertain a fantasy of heaven in which these ghosts would welcome the dog and take him running across that unbroken expanse of impersonal blue.

The mythologist Joseph Campbell has suggested that myth-making began with the first awareness of death, with the shock that a spirit could exist and then exist no more. I think that that shock gave birth to purpose, setting man forth on his eternal struggle to rationalize the irrational. Myths made it possible to deny finality by perceiving death as a journey and a transformation, the departing spirit moving on to take the form of constellations in the heavens, nymphs in wind and water, death-defying heroes in immortal tales.

Would we go mad without such thoughts of heaven? Without our ghosts and dreams of immortality? Who can accept that spirit can be snuffed out as finally as flame? That life is little more than a tease, dangling creatures before us to whom we will proclaim our love in song and sonnet before they are snatched back midsentence, leaving us to stare, open-mouthed into space?

Yet, trained in skepticism, I am awkward when asking the vet for a lock of fur before cremation. I am reminded of the discovery, not long ago, of Neanderthal men buried in Alpine caves with the bones of the bears they had hunted. It is unsettling to find myself seeking warmth by the fires of the ancients, sitting on my haunches and staring heavenward.

On the night of our dog's death, I bake an apple pie, open three dozen oysters and a fine, chilly wine, unaware that I am preparing a wake. There is an aspect of ritual that is unconscious and automatic.

The family gathers about the table and begins to reminisce. Smiles spread above chins shiny with brine as we recall when our daughter was five and announced that she wanted to marry the dog. My mother, who has the grace not to laugh at children unless they're asking for a laugh, fashioned a wedding gown of old lace curtains. The barefoot bride, fresh from the playground and smelling sweetly of child's sweat, rested her knuckles on the furry head as I performed the ceremony before our makeshift altar, the bathtub. I omitted, "till death do us part," considering that sounded too ominous for a child, and knowing that to own a dog is to deny that our life expectancy charts rarely merge. Unless you wait to become an owner when you are a 61.5-year-old male or 68.3-year-old female.

We recall when we first met the dog, opening our arms to capture the enthusiastic thrusts of sinew and bone, to hold him and make him ours. We conjure up that wild rush of life. It seems like yesterday, replacing yesterday in fact, a day of illness and worry. We have fulfilled the purpose of a wake.

In the days that follow, each of us feels the conflicting urge to tell the news and to hold grief unto ourselves. I want to tell strangers. I want to tell the man who sells me fish. As if saying the words will make it real. Just as for children, learning to speak lifts life out of a dream state into the light of day. But for sudden, unexpected moments when there is the surprise of tears, the death of this dog does not seem real. The lock of golden fur still reflects light.

I have felt a kinship with those ancients who made their peace with life by denying the finality of its end. Although I may not share their firm belief in heavenly transport, I too am unable to accept the extinguished spirit. I see it in the unthinking acts—the moment when I start to save table scraps, or ask the butcher for a bone, or the times when I reach into the remaining box of Milk-Bone and pull out a biscuit.

My housekeeper, long-widowed, once saw me stare at the betraying hand and said: "You know, Mrs. Ascher, it's just like people. Sometimes, I set a place at the table for my husband."

I know the dog is dead. I have the bill from the vet and the cancelled check to prove it. Conversations about him are in the past tense. Yet we can't believe that he's gone—*really* gone. We trip over the space he's left behind.

Depression Before Spring

> But ki-ki-ri-ki
> Brings no rou-cou,
> No rou-cou-cou.
> But no queen comes
> In slipper green.

WALLACE STEVENS

· ·

Her face is the color of whipping cream. The doctor tells me she lost a lot of blood during the hysterectomy. "Therefore," he mumbles through his mask, "we didn't take everything. The cervix was left behind."

Coming here, to visit my friend, I shared an elevator with jubilant fathers and grandmothers. They balanced packages gift wrapped in blues and pinks, and held the hands of young children who were discomfited by their new status as siblings. "Let me out of here!" one three-year-old boy screamed. His grandmother, smiling and preoccupied with her purchase and mission, straightened the blue ribbons on her gift and, in a manner common to adults in the company of the young, looked at us as she addressed the child. "You can't get out until we get to the fifth floor. That's where Mommy and your new baby brother are." She smiled at us, the other visitors, the elevator man, the nurses. Her grandson burst into tears. "But how will I get through all these people?" Then he got to the point. "There are too many people!"

"Brat," said a nurse as the doors closed and we left him wailing on the fifth floor. She had refused to return the grandmother's smile. "They never should have let children into the hospital," added a large woman with hair closely cropped, permed and hennaed to a rosy glow. She rolled her eyes. "They are completely out of place." The vehemence grew as we gained altitude. The elevator man tapped his temple with a dirty brown finger. "Loco," he said, turning to us. "It's the new administration. Loco." For some people, any administration is loco, and I suspected this was the case for this man.

On the eleventh floor I was released to make my way to the room of my friend who will never bring her children here against anyone's wishes. No eyes will roll as she departs. As of last night, there will be no children.

At thirty-nine, she had not yet married, finding no man a worthy rival of her solitude and career. They found the tumor before she found a mate.

The cells must be captured, she was told. An incision must be made to pursue and gather up the demons, to expose them to the light. Ovaries, fallopian tubes, and womb would be whisked away.

Some believe that if a woman has a soul, the womb is where

it resides. Whether or not it has housed the expanding partnership of sperm and egg, it is from there that the spirits speak. There are times when I have believed this. The Trobriand Islanders of Papua New Guinea have always believed this and hold that it is these womb spirits, rather than men, that impregnate women.

I have come to the hospital to replace silenced spirits with song, with a Walkman and a tape of Glenn Gould humming and soaring above a Bach partita. The doctors' eyes have already smiled above their masks and their muffled voices have announced the triumph, "No cancer!" She'll wonder why she's depressed, considering such good news. In ten days she will be released from this green room and returned to her apartment on Riverside Drive. She'll wonder, as she stares out the windows for the first week of a six-week confinement, did they scrape her skull as well? Visiting friends will reassure, "It's the anaesthesia. It muddles you. For every hour you were under, it takes a week to recover." They'll tell her, "Force fluids. Put up your feet. Don't rush it!"

Rush what? What do we mean? Don't push yourself, exhaust yourself, expect too much of yourself.

What's to expect? Rou-cou-cou will not answer ki-ki-ri-ki. No queen will come in slipper green.

Her hand, swollen and still, is raised on a pillow, the fingers poised as though on a keyboard. Beneath the yellow of their stretched skin are purple blotches left by the IV needle. She sighs and closes her eyes. The fingers relax.

It is silent here, high above Manhattan. I start the music and put the earphones on her head. The muffled piano is the only sound, save for the rattling of a stainless steel cart outside the door and the squeak of a nurse's rubber soles against linoleum. And then the sound of her open-mouthed breathing as air rushes in to fill the space.

Bubbles, Dust, Quarks, and Quirks

....

The phone rings. "Is your husband there?"

It's his tennis partner. I look at the clock, 9 A.M., he should have been on the court by now. The simple question is like a stone hitting calm water. The ripples spread out through my barely wakened morning consciousness. "No, he's not here. He left forty-five minutes ago. He ought to be there by now." The caller's voice adopts the reassuring tone of one who inadvertantly has caused alarm, "Well, then, I'm sure he'll be here any moment."

"I don't understand why he's not there," I say, and add

without thinking, as though still in dreams, "I don't understand love at all." I think I'm about to cry before good sense and strict upbringing stop the nonsense. After all, women send their men into space, I tell myself.

I am forty-two. I've been married to this man for half my life. We probably fit neatly into some wedge of the marital statistic pie. But what is behind those facts is not included in the shaded triangle of the graph entitled, "still together." What are the necessary components for the survival of love? Nobody knows. There are some theories about survival in general. We look to shipwrecks, natural disasters, and Arctic explorations to determine why some perish and others do not.

We learn from the sad fate of the 1845 Arctic expedition of Sir John Franklin and his 138 men that sterling silver flatwear is worthless when you've nothing left to eat but the ice you sit upon. We also know that it helps if you have a little extra body fat. One of the only two survivors of a high school class that recently climbed Mount Hood and was buried by an avalanche was a "husky fellow" according to his physician. The other had an "iron will," according to his parents. And that's about all the good the studies do us. The iron will that might save you on Mount Hood could be just the thing to destroy love.

Of course one hears the happy advice offered by celebrants at fiftieth wedding anniversary parties, but in fact no one has devised a method for predicting or measuring the survival of love. No thermometer has been invented to detect when its temperature has reached the level at which it freezes. When blood freezes it will not flow. There's no handy kit of emergency supplies to grab as you abandon your sinking ship and await rescue. Survival in the everyday sense goes unnoticed. Unless you're involved in transcendental meditation, who notices breathing? Unless you wear a pacemaker, who notices heartbeats? It was the waiting tennis partner's call that made me "catch" my breath, "feel" my heart as it gave a sudden thump against my chest cavity. Only the awareness of the possibility of loss makes one aware of the possibility of survival.

Rushes of adrenalin remind us. A step off the curb in front of an oncoming car. A child falling off a horse and, for a moment, catching her heel in the stirrup so that her head hangs between hoof and earth. A plane's sudden loss of altitude.

Close calls. Close calls remind us that we are here on the edge of loss. Sometimes I feel as if I'm on the outside rim of the orbiting earth, holding on by my fingertips while my legs fly out into the void, a void that physicists tell us is full of the wonders of bubbles, dust, quarks, and quirks.

Perhaps it's all a quirk. Who lives. Who dies. Who's born to abusive parents, who to adoring ones. Who lives in Colombia near a volcano, who is born into a village at the base of the Italian Alps that has sun only two months of the year. Who's born with a sunny, outgoing disposition that brings forth a positive response in others. Who is in the wrong place at the wrong time, at the ticket counter where the terrorist tosses the bomb. Who's in the right place at the right time when the person one is to love is there and ready to love in return.

Close calls. They wake us from our slumbers and shock us into an awareness of how supremely alive we are, and how simple it is to be severed from that life. Survival is a much more complicated issue than its opposite. I know from survival stories how easy it is, when hounded by fear and hunger, to step outside your tent into the Arctic winds, to lie down in the snow, to sleep. No sooner has the frost begun to gather on your beard than you're gone. Who has the fight, the spirit of say, Sir Ernest Shackleton, to struggle against such promised peace? What can we possibly learn from a man whose journey on foot across South Georgia Island has never been duplicated? The terrain is impassable, say those who have since tried and failed. One such adventurer described it as "a saw-tooth thrust through the tortured upheaval of mountain and glacier that falls in chaos to the northern sea." All that Shackleton's biographer, Alfred Lansing, can tell us is "there was no choice." A year and a half after his ship was imbedded in almost one million square miles of ice in the Weddell Sea, the journey was the only remaining hope of rescue.

Before setting out, Shackelton reduced his gear to the minimum. Three days of rations, a compass, binoculars and a page ripped from the Book of Job with the phrase, "Out of whose womb came the ice?"

Which of these was the key to survival?

Which page from the Bible should we clutch as we make our own determined marches across the "tortured upheaval" of dark nights? There are times, I think, when it might be easier to be free of the demands of love. Free of love's insistence that we be alive, that we feel, that we have the courage to follow the promptings of our hearts. There are times when it would be more peaceful to lie down quietly, alone in the cold, to let the snow gather, to surrender to wind and ice. What keeps us from that sleep is a mystery.

It's much more of a mystery than we like to think. After all, where would the science section of *The New York Times* be if we couldn't chart a course? What use sextants, loran, and radar? What would become of grants if we accepted that there's no way to predict the course of love running smooth?

What use sociologists, psychologists, social workers if they couldn't point out a few simple guidelines to keeping love alive?

We're an odd lot. We long for love, but resist a commitment to the unpredictable. We want statistics and formulas and yet we look to the most ephemeral sources for promises and predictions. It appears that a growing number look to the stars (Nancy Reagan was not alone), tea-leaf readers and practitioners of New Age philosophy. Tell me what's going to happen, we demand. We don't want to be caught off guard. We want to be prepared.

But love catches us off guard and unprepared. There we are on Mount Hood with nothing but blue jeans and sneakers when the snow begins to fall. There we are crossing the Canadian Arctic, running out of food and clutching our sterling silver flatwear, monogrammed with the family crest. Here we are on the edge of the void with nothing but our beating hearts.

The Widow Watchers

When I fell in love with an older man, it was not by design.
This was not a turn that I, and certainly not one that my
parents, had envisioned for the smooth and steady, determined path of my life.

There had been such worthy contenders who would have
fit into the scheme of things, back then when we thought
there was a scheme of things. One boy, a student at Exeter,
three years my senior and full of promise was handsome,
athletic, smart, and self-contained. The backs of his hands

were covered with golden fur. He was a golden boy. There was the gentle heir to a family food fortune. He danced with me when I was fourteen when no one else would. There were the young men on the list my family had provided the director of social events at my boarding school. They were allowed to come of a Sunday and sit on maroon plush in a dusty parlor. A chaperone sat nearby, oblivious to the blush spreading across my chest. Making conversation in that setting was probably good training for future wives of diplomats or traders in pork bellies.

There were blind dates in college—frenetic, determined, and fruitless. I wanted to share my soul, most of my dates had something else in mind. I wanted a husband and babies, even then. Why didn't they laugh me right out of their fraternity houses and eating clubs when I, deadly serious, would ask my date about his philosophy of life? Or when, against the strains of "Twist and Shout," I would seriously explain my belief in the sanctity of virgin brides.

I was so burdened, then, by who I was that although small and slight, I felt heavy with the imagined weight of my hands, my feet, my face, and my stomach that was always in a knot. I wanted someone to relieve me of the burden of myself, and the twenty-year-olds I met weren't up to that. How could they be?

And so, the man who made me feel as light as a feather was the man who had my heart. The man who wanted to read my poetry and hear my thoughts, and finally the man who held my hand and took away some of its weight.

But, it was not what I had planned, and so as he lightened my gravity, so I gravely continued my search for the boy who was meant to be my husband. For the boy whose manhood I thought I could somehow divine.

I have seen many an eye roll when conversation turns to second and third "younger" wives. Home wreckers, sirens, brazen hussies, the wanton ones whose wiles won the man away from a steadfast wife of a certain age. It's as if marriage were bound by the firm muscle tone of upper thighs and the woman with the least cellulite gets the man. Wins the knight in shining armor. In our thoughts about love and marriage we have not progressed far beyond the fairy tale. In these modern-day tales, men are helpless before the irresistible pull of youth. One could be led to believe that all it takes is the erect nipple of a younger breast to pierce the veil of marital bliss.

And, mind you, it is married men and women who would have us believe this, and perhaps have even convinced themselves of it. Men and women who know that marriage is cradled by such an intricate and complex web that its unravelling is beyond the comprehension of those who have woven it, let alone those on the outside accused of the unravelling.

But like fairy tales, these simplistic beliefs in external danger serve a purpose. They are ways of explaining the inexplicable. When a marriage is falling apart, it feels as though the earth is opening beneath your feet. As you slip through, and a passerby asks, "What happened?" it's impossible to say. But for those who feel inclined, or for some odd reason obliged to answer, it's easier to respond "He fell in love with a younger woman" than it is to outline the delicate fissures that weakened what held you.

It simplifies things. The younger woman, on the other hand, wishes that love had been simpler. Had not, from the start, been threatened by time. Of course, all of us are terminal, and there's that old reassuring standby, "You could be run over by a bus tomorrow." But the fact is, that as the younger wife takes her vows there is a loud ticking in her ears and it becomes as much a part of her as the ring that's placed on her finger. It is the sound of the clock set in motion by the union of two life expectancies that don't balance.

The conversation among younger wives is not like that of other women. There are the occasional attempts at black humor and reassurance. "When we're widows together . . ." one friend said before outlining hollow plans for trips to Patagonia. Trips to the ends of the earth. Trips to match the sense that, when left alone, one will fall off the edge of the world.

Another friend, blond and vital and forty years younger than her husband, determined, on the eve of his triple bypass surgery, that she must divorce him. It was only after the success of the procedure and his healthy recovery that she was able to say, "I realize my terrible anger was not at him or our lives, but at the possibility that he might die. I was going to leave him before he left me."

I have had such moments. I have wished that someone young would come to claim me. It's hard to remember that you can't have everything when love makes gluttons of us all. We determine that given this magic, surely we can make anything happen. Given this power, why should we be powerless? It is hard to come to terms with the fact that love comes to us the way it comes without conditions or cash bonuses at Christmas.

Upon the deaths of their husbands, many widows I know become like children. Most grow up and out of it, some do not. I've been watching them ever since I was married twenty-one years ago. I watch them the way we associates used to watch the partners in my law firm, trying to imagine what life would be like when we were one of them. The difference is that widowhood, unlike partnership, is nothing to aspire to. But I study them to see how they survive. I study them in order to be prepared.

"But look at how unexpected life's events are," a playwright married to an older man tells me, and points, as an example of life's capricious ways, to a thirty-five-year-old father we know who was jogging on the beach one day and the next was told he had incurable cancer. There is no planning, she tries to tell me, life will do to us what it will.

Of course, she does not believe this any more than I do. If we believed that life would have its way with us, we wouldn't be crying out against chaos. We wouldn't write, wouldn't go to the blank page determined that order could emerge from the random acts of our days. Words are the whips with which we tame the wild beasts of fear. We truly believe that we can whip life into shape.

And yet, we wild animal tamers are suckers for love. Despite our love of order, we love our children, disorderly in their whims and passions. We love them in spite of their refusal to follow life plans, in spite of the fact that all around us we see dropouts from family life, adult women estranged from their mothers, grown-up sons whose entire motivation in life is to be unlike their fathers. We get married in spite of the divorce rate. We fall in love, giving up our hearts and souls gladly, even though the widows remind us of our hearts' possible destination. And we do it because of the power that comes with love, a belief that no harm can come to hearts that beat with such passion. The enemies—separation and abandonment—will not get past the barriers of our devotion. People in love believe that they are unique. This child I begot will be smart and loyal and we will love each other. This person in whose arms I seek comfort and delight will hold me forever, just so. But even as we say it, we suspect it may be more wish than fact. Fate can be as devastating and mindless as a dinosaur's foot. Archeologists may find the prints in thousands of years and try to tell the tale. They too will make order out of chaos, sense out of the insensible. It's the stubborn, bullheaded human condition.

And so, of course, we who are married to older men, think we can prepare ourselves for grief, that we can arm ourselves beforehand. I know some who are doing so by turning their husbands away as the noticeable signs of age set in. "Every time he looks tired or old, I become so angry," a friend tells me. She becomes angry even as she knows her life was saved by falling in love with this man and by daring to have his baby. She is furious at the odds against her husband's attending their daughter's wedding some twenty years from now. Graduations, weddings, births, baptisms, our children's passages are the events by which we measure time and triumph.

When I was in love and twenty-one, I boldly told myself, "All I ask is twenty years with this man." Now that I've had twenty years, I'm grateful that fate wasn't listening, waiting to grant my wish. Twenty years is nothing, it's just enough time to begin to get the hang of it. The hang of loving. The hang of being loved. The hang of grace together.

We are the widow watchers, we young women married to older men. "Control freaks," one of our members claims. We want to settle the dust and change the furniture and prepare ourselves for what appears to be inevitable loss. "I will never be like . . ." she mentions two women we know, "living alone in their castles. Never." I promise myself not to be like another, a recent widow, who has become as small and wistful as a child. She has rid herself of all fat and dines only on dry toast and black coffee. Her voice has taken on the tone of a two-year-old so that no matter what her words, what she is saying is, "Don't hurt me. Take care of me. I am alone in the world. I am helpless." Does she starve herself to achieve some form of half death? To move closer to her deceased husband? I promise myself I will never be so helpless. Control freak. My friend is right. What a conceit to fancy that we will be in control when the earth drops out from under us.

A lot of widows go to China. Even the timid among us, even those who never left their hometown, are buying tickets for the next tour out. My husband's grandmother, when widowed, announced, "I have always wanted to go to Soviet Russia," and she booked herself a berth on a steamer. This was in 1937 when it was not unusual for a woman at her station in life to stay home and play whist, both before and after bereavement. It's enough to make you wonder how many years she had longed to climb on board. For how many years she had dreamed of Leningrad, Siberia, the Caucasus, while making small talk over tea sandwiches quartered and crustless.

The shy eighty-five-year-old mother of a friend of mine was recently widowed after forty years of marriage to a tyrannical man. Three weeks after his death, her daughter called, as she regularly does on Mondays at five. "Well, it's a good thing you called, you almost missed me," her mother announced.

"Missed you? Where are you going?"

"I'm leaving tomorrow for Australia." Leaving her farm in Ohio for the first time in forty years. "I'll call you when I get back."

"Well, when will that be?" asked my friend.

"Oh, I don't know. A month, maybe two. It depends . . ."

When a United Parcel Service man rang the doorbell and interrupted the call, the daughter was still astounded. She told him the story. "Oh, that's nothing," said he, handing her a receipt to sign. "When my father died two years ago, my eighty-year-old mother took up diving. You know, diving from a high board into a swimming pool? You ought to see her. Why, she just cuts through that water like a knife."

Cuts through the water like a knife. That's what I'd like to do. Become a high diver or a slalom racer. I'd like to look back over my snowy trail and witness the tracks of perfectly executed turns in white powder. Deep blue against white, a declaration of my control in descent.

I'll go to the snow when my time comes. Go to the snow and be so blinded by the sun at high altitudes, so frozen by temperatures below zero, that the coldness of my heart will be mistaken for a passing chill. Something brought on by weather and altitude. There will be warmth and relief at the bottom, I'll tell myself. A fire. A room. A frozen glass of grappa. I will confuse my heart with my toes and wonder as they thaw and sting and burn and return to themselves why my heart doesn't do likewise.

They Write Letters
to the Dead

....

They write letters to the dead. Every day on the obituary page of *The New York Times,* survivors' words go forth under the heading "In Memoriam." They speak of pain that never ends: "It's twenty years today, and you are still missed." They speak in poetic code that only the deceased could decipher: "Yellow Bird. Nothing gold can stay."

A friend, a pragmatic, no-nonsense English woman, occasionally places a long-distance call to Marie, a woman in Tulsa, "whose specialty is chatting with the dead." Marie has told my friend, among other things, that her deceased grand-mother "is very angry about that Wedgwood bowl. She wants you, not your mother, to have it." "My grandmother hated my mother," my friend explains.

For myself, I would prefer an end that is dark, final, and unremitting rather than such pettiness. Such news makes the afterlife sound like an endless beach gathering, day in, day out with the same small group, ingrown and riddled with gossip. It sounds like the worst of Bloomsbury.

We do, I suppose, each carry with us a notion of heaven. And I would, more or less, like to chat with the dead. I would prefer it if they were, well, a little less dead. Even the most rational among us has stared intently at mummies in museums, attempting to make out the shape of the corpse beneath the wrappings. Has stared, waiting for the blink of an eye or the heave of a chest that would send us running, screaming to the guard, "It's alive! It's alive!"

I remember an interview with Ethel Kennedy during which she is purported to have stated that she would never remarry because, with Bobby looking down from heaven, that would be adultery.

I hope the dead are not looking down from heaven or fussing over fidelity and Wedgwood bowls. That would make them like members of a small town church congregation. That would make them the same inhibiting force that God and Santa Claus were in our childhoods. The business of naughty or nice should be left to the living.

I like the Southern expression "passed over." In Mississippi you'll hear that "Mr. Joseph passed over a year ago today." Crossed the River Jordan, more benign than the Styx. A gentle journey to another plane. Crossed over, never to return. So much the better, I say.

When I was six years old, Elizabeth Taylor threw herself onto Mike Todd's grave. Or did I imagine it? There was no comforting her. The news came over the radio into our kitchen where I sat on the floor playing jacks. I was rivetted by the notion of passion out of control. Such things never happened in our corner of New England.

No. In our community death was a quiet and shameful thing. You hid it from sight as soon as possible. No open casket. No wake. No announcement. But the news travelled and adults showed up at the graveside. It was, after all, another joyless task in the pursuit of doing what was "right." It was their civic duty to the survivors. When I was in fifth grade, a classmate died, and according to his family's tradition, his body was driven past the places he had inhabited. This brought the cortege past the playground during recess. We froze and fell silent, before we giggled and made a joke of it. When his older brother returned to school, bearing a look of shame and what we imagined to be the scent of death, we banished him from our ranks.

Unlike my friend who calls the lady in Tulsa, unlike the strangers who write letters in memoriam, I don't think that children, under any circumstances, wish to talk to the dead. For them the dead are fearful things—ghouls, goblins, and monsters that make sounds in the night.

It is only with time that the dead grow benign. As we grow older, as there is more to fear that is real and in our midsts, as we become both more and less the masters of our own fates, we move closer to those "dearly departed." We want to know something about the end of this journey. We visit graveyards, we read the obituary columns. We want to know, how goes it?

It was not until the age of thirty that I found the idea of

heaven acceptable. In the past, Easter was the one celebration in my church, the central celebration, which I found morbid and frightening. A time of tombs and caves, rolling rocks and weeping women. I remained among the faithful by avoiding the main issue.

My grandmother's death changed all that. I had loved her with mindless passion and the favor had been returned. She had been gentle with my shyness, soothing the sharp angles of my young body and easing my shame when angles softened into curves. For a woman of such love and gentleness, I longed for a gentle place. A place where we could meet again. And yes, I even hoped that she would look down, because hers was a loving glance.

I would write a letter to her if I believed the dead could read. I'd write a letter and send the check to *The New York Times* so that they would print it. I'd write a letter to fill in the blanks left by my tongue-tied, earthly love.

Going Away,
Coming Home

....

There it is, I can see it from the plane, Prospero's island rising in the mist. Will it be there when our plane descends or will it have "melted into air, into thin air?" I believe anything is possible, so held in place am I by a sense of home, so set on the edge of fear. To be attached is to fear loss. What if? What if?

Each winter, as we approach this tropical island, making our annual pilgrimage to shake off January's drafty malaise, to see the light, it is with the sense of a dream coming true, and the companion fear that "we are such stuff as dreams are made on." When we step out into the sun, we rub our eyes, less from its brightness than to erase sleep and images of snow from our eyes, to reassure ourselves that it is real. Yes, we are really home.

How to explain why we feel at home here. We don't own it, there is no deed, no covenant running with the land. No easements. No encumbrances. We are here only ten days a year. We find it difficult to understand the native tongue, and the climate is foreign to our New England natures. But when we first arrived, seventeen years ago, we knew it was right. Like love at first sight, or putting on a favorite pair of well-worn slippers after a hard day out in the world. Like holding your child's hand as you sit in a darkened movie house watching Fred Astaire and Ginger Rogers make your world complete with a pas de deux. To feel at home is to feel like your best self. That self capable of joy and the ease of being. That's how we feel at this resort in the British Virgin Islands.

We aren't the only ones. "My dear," a Guccied, departing matron tells me, "your seventeen years are nothing. We've been coming for twenty-four." Home does that. It brings out one's primitive sense of territory. If you look around, we could be so many lions leaving our scent. Each of us is announcing, "This is mine." Newcomers are to be distrusted. To this lady making her twenty-fourth departure, I am a newcomer.

But not as new as that couple down the beach who is unaware that we do not play paddleball here. Nor do we call out to one another. The silence of a cathedral is to be interrupted only by song. Here it is the song of the banaquit, the kingbird, the pearly-eyed thrasher.

There are plenty of transients, those who speak of last year at Curtain Bluff and next year in Jerusalem, who like their vacations spiced with adventures of the unknown. It all depends which part of the psyche needs soothing.

My working mind demands adventure. Just give me twenty-four-hour notice and nothing pleases me more than to head for the jungle, the pampas, the ice. Drop me down among strangers. It sharpens my senses and soothes the muse. But for vacation, I am drawn to places steeped in memory. Thomas Mann was right, the memory is a well, and I long to dip into past joys, observations, moments of tender and arrested attention. The kind of attention of which the vacating mind is capable.

When I walk from the beach to the house, I walk with ghosts of the past. My late friend Cam McVey is always beside me as I pass the tamarind tree where we stood, not daring to breathe lest we frighten the great blue heron poised in its shade. When I look at the stars, I see more than Cassiopeia, I see Bill Chandler who taught me how to find it. His wife Louise's voice of propriety is in my ear whenever I see behavior in the dining room "unbecoming" the ladies and gentlemen who originally came to this place.

Home is a place where you can fill your days with happy remembrance. The moment we step over the threshold of our room, year after year, there is more than the sound of the cuckoo on the hill and the waves on the reef. There is a symphony of past birdsong, past surf, and the echoes of goats that once came to graze before an urban guest complained to the management.

We greet the wildlife as one would greet household pets after an absence. "There's our hawk!" There it is, in fact, on its usual perch, the peak of the dining pavillion. Twisting its head to the bay, to the mountains behind, to the gardens of hibiscus, jasmine, frangipani, and century plants falling away to either side. The rising sun casts its breast feathers in bronze, and the moon lingers at its back like a guest refusing to take the hint that the party's over. Is it the same bird, or a descendent? I don't know the way of hawks, but I do know that it is these small, repetitive gestures of nature that reassure.

I am charmed, as I am every year, by the eyes in the back of the bird's head, a feathered deception. It would be fine to live like that hawk. To sit on a high place with breezes lifting the feathers and caressing the skin. To have eyes in the back of the head. To know your place and never have to leave.

But the fact of departure may impart the poignance to our arrivals. Like lovers meeting for clandestine hours, each moment is savored, no sense is ignored. We live a triple life. The life of memory, the life of the moment, and an extra life for the future's memories. Squirreling away each day's experiences, a feast to uncover when we return to the lean days of remaining winter. We are as richly alive as children, those natural nostalgics, whose earliest conversations are full of "Remember when . . . ," who take stock of existence with the watchful eye of the poet and begin to weave the web of memory that will cradle them in old age.

On vacation, I like to go home. To return to those places so steeped in memory that to step ashore is to step into Mann's well and float through the wet and wondrous ways of days gone by while my head is warmed by today's sun. On vacation, all I ask is a sense of forever.

PAYING
HEED

On Power

....

When I graduated from law school, I was hired by what is known in the business as a Prestigious New York Law Firm. I felt privileged to be associated with talent and money and respectability, to be in a place that promised me four weeks vacation, my own secretary, an office with a window, and, above all, a shot at power. I would not have preferred working for a single practitioner who struggled to pay rent on his windowless, one-room office in the Bronx.

There's a lot to be said for the accouterments of power.

Those who asked where I worked immediately assumed, upon being told the name of the firm, that I must have been at the top of my class, an editor of the Law Review and a clerk for a federal judge. I was none of these, but being where the power is frees you from having to explain yourself.

The "outsider's" version of the "insider" is always distorted by the mental glass through which they observe. The outsider tends to think that once inside the power structure the voyage is over, destination reached. No more struggle or strain. But in fact, once you have "arrived," you discover that there are power structures within the power. You may share office space and a central switchboard, but that doesn't mean you are at the controls.

In my firm, the partners (male) took the young associates (also male), resplendent in their red suspenders and newly sported cigars, to lunch, to Dallas, Los Angeles, and Atlanta to meet the clients. The "girl" associates were sent to the library to do research. Actually, they were sent to the library to stay out of trouble.

Soon the clients with whom the associates dined were calling them for advice. These associates were learning how to practice law. Those of us hidden away in the stacks were learning how to be invisible.

A friend at a similar Prestigious New York Law Firm told me that she had tried and failed to enlist the cooperation of the one woman partner. "I suggested that we, the women associates and she, have monthly luncheons to discuss some of the problems we faced. After all, she'd been one of us." But she was no longer "one of us" and feared that if her partners perceived her as an ally of women associates, they might forget that she was, first and foremost, one of "them." She knew that hanging out with weak sisters was no way to safeguard her tentative grasp of success.

Eight years later, when my friend became a partner, she learned that the woman she had approached for help was powerless within the partnership. She was, in the eyes of the men, their token "girl" partner, and power, like beauty, is in the eye of the beholder. She was a lady and that's how she was perceived. How could her mother have known as she trained her daughter for power in the drawing room that what she would want was power in the boardroom?

However, even if hers was a token acceptance, she had entered that heady realm, she was feted around town as "the first woman partner" and she proceeded to follow a pattern not unusual for women who achieve some semblance of power. She refused to reach behind to pull other women along. It was too risky. She might fall backwards. I blush to recall that when, in fourth grade I was the only girl on the boys' baseball team, I joined in their systematic "girl trashing." I enthusiastically participated in disparaging conversations about people who were "just girls." Who threw like girls. Who giggled like girls. Who couldn't whistle through their fingers, burp on command or slide into home plate. Then, all I knew was that my power depended on keeping other girls out. Now, I know about identification with the aggressor.

Not that it makes much difference. There are uncanny similarities between being the only girl on a fourth grade baseball team and the only woman in bigger boys' games. Take, for instance, the response of Harvard Business School's tenured, female professors when their former colleague, Barbara Bund Jackson, filed suit against the school for its refusal to grant her tenure. Nonsense, these women replied to Jackson's charge of a sexist "institutional bias." Not so, they said of her contention that the school sets "impossible standards for female faculty members." Why shouldn't they? Why should Harvard deviate from the accepted wisdom that a man can occasionally goof off and still be perceived as powerful? It's kind of cute, we say. Oh, look, he's got nice human touches, an ability to have fun. How boyish. How charming. Not so for a woman. She who goofs off is a goof-off.

Tenured Harvard professor Regina E. Herzlinger's response to Jackson's claim of discrimination was, "I don't feel there is . . . friction caused by the fact that there are few women on the faculty . . . I don't think there is discrimination on the basis of sex." Of course there isn't friction for those "few women." And Regina'd better keep quiet if she thinks otherwise. Boys don't like girls who turn around and say, "But what about the other girls?" I certainly never invited my friend Linda to play baseball with us, even though she ran like the wind and threw overhand.

But power, who has it and who doesn't, is not limited to the realm of male/female strife. My husband, a physician in practice for many years, volunteers his time, one day a week at a hospital often described with the same breathless reverence as my law firm. This is the place to which ailing shahs and wealthy dowagers come to be healed. The full time attendings (those with the power) don't like the voluntary attendings (those without the power), and occasionally rise up to divest them of responsibility. How, you might ask, when wise and seasoned physicians are willing to give their time, free of charge, to teach students and treat patients, could there be a complaint? The volunteers are not part of the power structure. And power's particular drive is to grab more for itself, an act which invariably involves stripping others of any.

Recently, some of the voluntary attendings went to the head of their department and informed him, "You make us feel like second-class citizens." He listened, nodded, and assured: "You are second-class citizens."

Irrational, you say? Of course. But whoever thought that the power drive made sense?

In fifth grade, secret clubs were the order of the day. The purpose was, first of all, the secret. A secret name. Secret rules. Secret members. Secret meeting places. The purpose was to exclude, which is the first step in establishing a power base. The second is to create fear in those excluded. Those of us who assembled the group of meanest and most popular children had the run of the playground. We were a force to contend with.

Recently, when I went to choose a puppy from a litter, I was told, "Don't get the Alpha dog, whatever you do!" It seems that, like their ancestors the wolves, each litter has a leader. He or she is the power in the pack, and once the Alpha dog comes to live with your family, you become the pack.

What does the Alpha dog get for his trouble? A certain haughtiness. A certain swagger. What did the Alpha attorneys in my firm get for their power? A certain haughtiness. A certain swagger. And an occasional invitation to the Piping Rock Country Club.

So who cares? We all did. We who sat in the library working on Blue Sky Memos, something my twelve-year-old daughter could have done, given the careful and patronizing instructions we received. We were enraged at being excluded from Making It Big. What we didn't know at the time is that the ones who Make It Big are always watching their backs, but then girls rarely have the opportunity to learn these finer points.

Power sanctions self-centeredness. (It could be argued that that's why girls don't have it—"They're so giving.") It returns you, full circle, to the delicious years of being an infant and toddler when, it seemed, you were the center of the universe. But what is missing at thirty-five, forty, or fifty years of age is the innocence of the infant, the two- or three-year-old. It is a dangerous absence. Self-interest plus muscle power and experience combine to create a being more pervasively harmful than the sandbox bully.

Take, for instance, Manhattan real estate developers. They are currently a favorite target of the less powerful, and are, in some instances, a legitimate target. There are those who use their amassed fortunes to gain political sway by contributing to the campaign funds of elected officials. The elected officials then turn deaf ears to the complaints of less powerful constituents dispossessed from low rent buildings razed to make room for luxury high rises complete with Jacuzzis in every bath.

Donald Trump's song of himself is on the best-seller lists. *Vanity Fair* featured a breathlessly infatuated profile of his wife. Why? Because if you can't be powerful, the next best thing is to fancy yourself on intimate terms with those who are. There is a hunger to know how they make their deals, shop for their children's Christmas presents, stay fresh and alert from five A.M. until Peter Duchin's orchestra plays its last charity ball waltz at midnight. All this, and not a wrinkle in the brow to show for it.

People read about power for the same reason that little girls read *Cinderella*, they want to believe that someday a prince will come to deliver a subject into sovereignty.

One might ask whether adulation of those who are flagrantly self-involved makes any sense when there are thousands of dispossessed sleeping in Grand Central and Pennsylvania Station. It certainly doesn't make mature sense.

But then power is not necessarily in mature hands. It is most often achieved, and clung to by those whose passion for it is fueled by childlike greed and self-interest. What they find, once they have it, is that being the proud possessor of power bears an uncanny similarity to being the two-year-old with the biggest plastic pail and shovel on the beach. It's a life of nervous guardianship.

I left the law because I wasn't motivated to engage in the struggle required to move myself from library to the light of day and lunches with clients. The struggle would have required molding myself in the partners' images, a hard concept for them to visualize since I was female and they were male. It would have been necessary to remember when to speak and when to keep my mouth shut. I would have had to create an asexual aura. I would have had to work very, very hard.

I left the law because that wasn't the power that interested me. Which is not to say that power itself doesn't interest me. I remember the full glory of being the only girl on the boy's baseball team. I remember the total sense of worthlessness that resulted when I grew breasts and the guys banished me from the pitcher's mound to the powerless world of hopscotch. Power is as tantalizing as a hypnotist's swinging pendulum. Power promises that you will never again be stuck with "the girls." Ask Regina Herzlinger. She knows.

On Parenting
and Consequence

....

On a cloudy August morning as we read of Jennifer Dawn
Levin, eighteen years old and lifeless on the grass in Central
Park, a bra pulled tight around her neck, we wondered where
our children were.

The mystery was that our children weren't wondering
where their parents were. Perhaps they'd grown accustomed
to our absences—absences not fully explained by affluence,
divorce, or the two-career family. The abandonment was
more than physical. It was emotional, spiritual, and complete.

It was as though the job of raising children, of "bringing them up" had become too difficult. Parents wanted pals, not dependents. Harmony, not the raw emotions of questing children. They wanted to talk contraception, not character. If they wanted to talk at all.

"You have to understand," a senior at one of Manhattan's private schools explained, "parents travel a lot or work eighteen hours a day. But," she reassured, "they leave money." She told of a classmate for whom it was customary, upon returning home to an empty apartment, to find a hundred dollar bill and a note from her mother, telling her, "Away for a long weekend. Be good."

Be good. Did her mother know what that meant? Did the daughter? Do any kids? And if so, where do they learn? The parents say that's a lesson the schools ought to teach. But the schools say, as one teacher succinctly stated, "These kids come to us without a moral code and we can't teach it to them." She also confided, "The only thing that surprised me about the Levin murder was that the victim wasn't . . ." and named a girl well known for her sexual promiscuity.

Many adults had alternative victims in mind. And some mentioned young men they knew who were just as capable of violence as Levin's killer, Robert E. Chambers, Jr. Suddenly, it was as though evil had entered the wrong peoples' lives, and that the children were to blame. That they had allowed death and violence to cross some imagined rightful boundary. The ghetto, Central America, Lebanon.

What was it doing in these dining rooms, lapping about slippered feet as though the morning news had been borne in on a flood tide? The parents demanded to be taken to high ground, to have distance placed between their children and those of the Levins and the Chamberses. "Surely kids don't go into Central Park at night?" "Yes they do. All the time," the children answered. "Well, certainly not anyone you know." "Yes, lots of people I know."

Why, parents asked, had Knickerbocker Dance Classes, Knickerbocker Grays, Chapin, Brearley, Spence and their very own children failed to keep them safe? And what of the unspoken agreement between parents and children, that parents could be excused from parenting and children from consequence? Here was consequence, dead in the grass.

Why had it become important to parents that their children live lives of fiction? Had their own childhoods of demands, expectations, punishment, and rewards been so deprived that they were determined to spare the next generation? Did they resent being human all that much? So much that they would have their offspring believe that life could be just like TV? That blood spurted from capsules, not wounds, and that evil was something created in the imagination of a script writer. Good was what the star of the show got to be.

The result was that when real life intruded with stubborn insistence, children seemed slightly surprised, as if a hand had reached through the screen and chucked them under the chin. In photographs, Robert Chambers's unfocused eyes are those of a dazed child who has sat staring too long at Saturday morning cartoons. One who sits and stares at the screen even after the television has been turned off.

There was a time, once, when parents spoke of "building character." I think of my own father as one not atypical of his generation. His character had been "built" by strict standards of behavior and morality enforced by unswerving (today they would be termed "rigid") parents. His was not an easy childhood, informed as it was by delayed gratification and the hard lessons of self-control. He was expected to treat girls like ladies, and money as though there might be none tomorrow. Prudence and restraint, his father had said, were part of becoming a man.

What has become of those lessons of patience and fortitude? Without them, the children fail to learn that gratification can be postponed and nobody dies of it. That if it is not, somebody might.

And why have children been turned over to the mercy of two A.M. Manhattan streets and the cradling arms of peers? When did parents become frightened of forbidding demanded pleasure?

A friend recently informed me that when she banished one of her daughter's classmates for behavior "unacceptable under my roof," she received a call from the girl's mother who announced with rage, "Nobody does that to my daughter."

I'm sure she's right. There are few who react to evil with rejection, to bad behavior with a rap on the knuckles.

In the days following Jennifer Levin's death, parents turned against the children for having become the enemy of their illusions. They were repelled by the fact that the young they harbored were not the junior versions of Jamesian ladies and gentlemen the schools had been expected to create; rather, they were shockingly like themselves. Little lost boys for whom growing up promised only loss.

A father who withheld his son's allowance as punishment for being caught snorting cocaine in school had told me, several years before his son's infraction, "I can get anything I want on the floor" of the stock exchange. And his son soon learned that he could get anything he wanted out of his father's bureau drawer.

A mystified mother who returned home from Paris to find a depleted wine cellar, ashtrays full of half-smoked marijuana butts, and cigarette burns in a two-hundred-year-old Aubusson rug, later said to friends gathered for lunch, "I don't get it. We've never smoked pot in front of the kids. In fact, we've told them we're vehemently opposed. And furthermore, my husband and I only smoke one joint a night. To relax."

These stories abound. We tell the stories to bring us to an answer. And we tell the stories to distance ourselves. People refer to the Levin killing as "the Preppy murder," to mute the horror by trivializing both the victim and the killing instinct. To isolate the vulnerability of children to a particular social group. The truth is that there is not one of us, who, startled in the night by dreams or a sound in the street, does not lie awake and wonder where the children are. And then begin to wonder, where were we?

On Compassion

....

The man's grin is less the result of circumstance than dreams
or madness. His buttonless shirt, with one sleeve missing,
hangs outside the waist of his baggy trousers. Carefully plaited
dreadlocks bespeak a better time, long ago. As he crosses
Manhattan's Seventy-ninth Street, his gait is the shuffle of
the forgotten ones held in place by gravity rather than plans.
On the corner of Madison Avenue, he stops before a blond
baby in an Aprica stroller. The baby's mother waits for the
light to change and her hands close tighter on the stroller's
handle as she sees the man approach.

The others on the corner, five men and women waiting for the crosstown bus, look away. They daydream a bit and gaze into the weak rays of November light. A man with a briefcase lifts and lowers the shiny toe of his right shoe, watching the light reflect, trying to catch and balance it, as if he could hold and make it his, to ease the heavy gray of coming January, February, and March. The winter months that will send snow around the feet, calves and knees of the grinning man as he heads for the shelter of Grand Central or Pennsylvania Station.

But for now, in this last gasp of autumn warmth, he is still. His eyes fix on the baby. The mother removes her purse from her shoulder and rummages through its contents: lipstick, a lace handkerchief, an address book. She finds what she's looking for and passes a folded dollar over her child's head to the man who stands and stares even though the light has changed and traffic navigates about his hips.

His hands continue to dangle at his sides. He does not know his part. He does not know that acceptance of the gift and gratitude are what make this transaction complete. The baby, weary of the unwavering stare, pulls its blanket over its head. The man does not look away. Like a bridegroom waiting at the altar, his eyes pierce the white veil.

The mother grows impatient and pushes the stroller before her, bearing the dollar like a cross. Finally, a black hand rises and closes around green.

Was it fear or compassion that motivated the gift?

Up the avenue, at Ninety-first Street, there is a small, French bread shop where you can sit and eat a buttery, overpriced croissant and wash it down with rich cappuccino. Twice when I have stopped here to stave hunger or stay the cold, twice as I have sat and read and felt the warm rush of hot coffee and milk, an old man has wandered in and stood inside the entrance. He wears a stained blanket pulled up to his chin, and a woolen hood pulled down to his gray, bushy eyebrows. As he stands, the scent of stale cigarettes and urine fills the small, overheated room.

The owner of the shop, a moody French woman, emerges from the kitchen with steaming coffee in a Styrofoam cup, and a small paper bag of . . . of what? Yesterday's bread? Today's croissant? He accepts the offering as silently as he came, and is gone.

Twice I have witnessed this, and twice I have wondered, what compels this woman to feed this man? Pity? Care? Compassion? Or does she simply want to rid her shop of his troublesome presence? If expulsion were her motivation she would not reward his arrival with gifts of food. Most proprietors do not. They chase the homeless from their midst with expletives and threats.

As winter approaches, the mayor of New York City is moving the homeless off the streets and into Bellevue Hospital. The New York Civil Liberties Union is watchful. They question whether the rights of these people who live in our parks and doorways are being violated by involuntary hospitalization.

I think the mayor's notion is humane, but I fear it is something else as well. Raw humanity offends our sensibilities. We want to protect ourselves from an awareness of rags with voices that make no sense and scream forth in inarticulate rage. We do not wish to be reminded of the tentative state of our own well-being and sanity. And so, the troublesome presence is removed from the awareness of the electorate.

Like other cities, there is much about Manhattan now that resembles Dickensian London. Ladies in high-heeled shoes pick their way through poverty and madness. You hear more cocktail party complaints than usual, "I just can't take New York anymore." Our citizens dream of the open spaces of Wyoming, the manicured exclusivity of Hobe Sound.

And yet, it may be that these are the conditions that finally give birth to empathy, the mother of compassion. We cannot deny the existence of the helpless as their presence grows. It is impossible to insulate ourselves against what is at our very doorstep. I don't believe that one is born compassionate. Compassion is not a character trait like a sunny disposition. It must be learned, and it is learned by having adversity at our windows, coming through the gates of our yards, the walls of our towns, adversity that becomes so familiar that we begin to identify and empathize with it.

For the ancient Greeks, drama taught and reinforced compassion within a society. The object of Greek tragedy was to inspire empathy in the audience so that the common response to the hero's fall was: "There, but for the grace of God, go I." Could it be that this was the response of the mother who offered the dollar, the French woman who gave the food? Could it be that the homeless, like those ancients, are reminding us of our common humanity? Of course, there is a difference. This play doesn't end—and the players can't go home.

On Danger

....

"I got out of Argentina by the skin of my teeth." That's how
I like to start the story every time.

"How was your trip?"

"Well, I have to admit, I got out by the skin of my teeth."

"Welcome home!"

"And none too soon, let me tell you."

"Barbara, I understand you were in Argentina."

"Was I ever!"

Dialogues in the days of safe return. Anyone who asked was

not told of golden pampas grass or the open and endless beauty that beckoned me each morning as I rode on horseback towards a horizon I never reached. I did not want my tale to be a travelogue or an Argentine version of "Flying Down to Rio." I had had an adventure and was striving to convey the sense of wonder, fear and self-reliance that results from setting forth alone in the world. Although I was not an Elizabethan explorer, I wanted my account to sound like the expeditions of Martin Frobisher. And thus I told my tale.

With every telling, I highlighted the incident that caused fear and then release from fear. Having driven out of mountain country to catch a flight back to Buenos Aires, I found the small airport surrounded by grim armed and uniformed men. All personnel and passengers were on emergency alert because bombs had exploded the previous evening outside an embassy (no one was hurt) and inside the home of a government official (who was elsewhere, in white tie and tails).

We were searched. Nightgowns, lacey underpants and dressing gowns were spilled across the counter. Broad hands explored their silky folds and no one blushed. Wiring of hair dryers was inspected. Shampoo bottles opened and sniffed.

Those around me shrugged. They'd lived through juntas. They'd lived through rebel takeovers. Guerrillas had held them hostage. They'd been told to leave the country to save their lives. "The bombs are simply the military's attempt to discredit the democratic government on the eve of elections," a fellow traveler explained and turned to talk of polo and the society page of the morning newspaper.

I thought of friends whose mothers had instructed them never to leave home with torn underwear lest, "You're run over by a car and taken to the hospital." I had always been curious about the mentality that could create a fantasy combining, with equal force, fear of fatality and the state of undergarments. Have modern mothers brought their advice up to date? Don't travel unmended lest the security guard unpack your bag. Lest a terrorist detain you.

Should mothers better equip their young for adventure? Give them Swiss army knives rather than sewing kits, canteens rather than little chintz bags in which to pack shoes. And instead of instructions in darning, should they demonstrate how to rub two sticks together to make a spark? Arm them with bravery rather than with precautionary tales. If you're crouched on an ice floe eating raw polar bear meat, courage is the only underpinning that must remain intact.

If you don't lay claim to danger, it will claim you. But we are so frightened that we hesitate to admit danger's existence, the first step in teaching courage. When we sense that danger is beyond our control, superstition becomes its foil. However, perfect tailoring will not keep drunken drivers at bay. Not letting our glances meet another's as we step onto the BMT downtown line will not prevent our being mugged. Listening for the sound of our returning young at night will not insure that they return at all.

I think I told my tale as I did, because although there was no real danger, merely inconvenience in our situation, I had sensed that to be touched by danger is to be, for that moment, more fully alive. I had wearied of "women and children first." Of being cast off in life's lifeboat to drift with the currents and await rescue.

We have known that something has been missing. Young people stay young longer than they used to. Older people don't see maturity as a goal necessarily worthy of their aspirations. What we were not certain of was that facing danger eye-to-eye and staring it down is an important step in becoming more fully adult. The danger of which I speak is not to be confused with that created by wandering subway marauders, drunken drivers, or fatal illnesses, things which force themselves upon and victimize us. I am speaking of danger on which we force ourselves, our skills, and cunning.

You can have it for a price. You can be put on an island and told to forage for a week. Or taken into the mountains and dropped off with hook, line, and sinker. Many affluent parents of the late sixties and seventies sent their adolescent children on such programs. "To find themselves." A month-long character reformation, drug cleanup, and "possible sexual initiation," one mother of the time told me. It was odd how these kids, pried from Saturday morning TV, Wednesday night sitcom, and country club tennis lessons, were expected to return home with the personalities and forbearance of Arctic explorers. The truth is, they came home and turned on the television.

They were not equipped with an Arctic explorer's dream, or sense of mystery and mission. They did not share the compulsion, central to his calling, to test themselves against the most formidable forces of nature. If you have read Annie Dillard's essay, "An Expedition to the Pole," you understand that nineteenth-century Arctic explorers ventured forth to meet their souls on ice. We no longer go exploring because we don't know what to look for.

I want to meet my soul on ice, but fear that should I spot it staring at me from a neighboring floe, I might not recognize it, I might aim my camera and ask it to pose with the penguins.

And yet, we are not so unlike the nineteenth century explorers, we have a sense that the pathway to self-knowledge is one of high adventure. There are travel organizations based on that premise. Before the public discovered that riding a space shuttle was not the same as riding a city bus, I received a call from the president of a tour organization asking if I would like to go, as a writer, free-of-charge, into space in 1990. "You'd better let us know soon," I was told. "We're almost completely booked." When I thanked him for thinking of me, but let him know that I preferred earthly adventures, he responded with renewed enthusiasm, "We've got an awfully nice package to the North Pole. Weather permitting."

Weather there is never permitting. Your feet come off with your socks and you might have to eat your dogs. But people have signed up and are ready to go, any day now.

In other words, they have chosen their danger rather than being its passive victim. Perhaps this is what inspired Christa McAuliffe to volunteer for space. Yet, in the end, for all her daring she was a passive victim. Once strapped into the seat of the space shuttle, there was nothing within her skill, training, or instinct for survival that could have made her the mistress rather than the passenger of her destiny.

I long for that heroic moment that can only be found on the edges of danger where one's skill makes all the difference. That moment that reveals oneself. I envy Beryl Markham who flew west with the night across the Atlantic in 1936 with nothing to contemplate but the size of her "small courage." And Sir Ernest Shackleton, the British Antarctic explorer, described by Alfred Lansing in *Endurance* as "an explorer in the classic mold—utterly self-reliant, romantic, and just a little swashbuckling." I'd like to be just a little swashbuckling. To be among those who, in navigating danger, with courage, passion and knowledge as their only instruments, absolutely know themselves.

Every swashbuckling act of that adventurer Odysseus was informed by passion. Passion for home, son, servants, his men and, of course, Penelope. It propelled him against the forces of angry gods, monsters, and scorned lovers. It inspired his triumphant attacks on the dangers that beset him. It prevailed, a life force stronger than those sent to challenge it.

Who could not envy such passion? Who would not fear it? Do we really want to be so open to experience that we must be tied to a mast or confronted by the Cyclopes who "care not a jot for Zeus with his aegis, nor for the rest of the blessed gods, since we are much stronger than they." Or the Laestrygonians "in their thousands-huge fellows, more like giants than men."

No. Instead, we hover in the corners of our homes, shaking with the fears that we feel unable to vanquish. Without true adventure, without the opportunities to pit ourselves against the real dangers it presents, we are not equipped to face the fears delivered by the mundanity of daily life. Fear that a child won't be accepted at the nursery school of choice; fear of the bank statement; fear of angering a friend, ending a relationship, beginning a relationship, lack of success and success itself. All of these become the Cyclopes of our lives. Our fantasies become the Laestrygonians, "more like giants" than what they really are. Bêtes noires, not the true beasts.

Every hero has had his beasts to conquer. Beowulf his Grendel. Shackleton his Antarctic winter. A beast that, in the moment of contact, inspired his enemy to be his most alive and passionate self. Every hero shook in his boots and felt his pounding heart. I want to feel my pounding heart. Not perch in a lifeboat, mending my underwear, as I watch the circling sharks.

On Trust

....

My friend tells me that when she was an adolescent, she
discovered that her mother read her mail and listened to her
phone calls. "I think that she even read my diary," she says,
and gasps. "Oh, my God, what if she . . . she wouldn't have
. . . yes, she would have." She sinks back into the chair and
covers her eyes with her hands. Twenty-five years after the
fact, she assumes the posture of a child shamed and says,
"When I was seventeen, and still living at home, I had my
first sexual encounter. Of course I wrote about it in my diary,

because there was no one else. . . . So, I just tried to sort it all out by writing about it." She sighs as she remembers, "I probably wrote about the entire thing. . . . Oh, my God, I'll never be able to look her in the eye again."

It's the mother's gaze that should be averted by shame. It is the mother, not the daughter who committed criminal trespass, if not in the legal sense, then certainly in the familial and ethical sense. But children, of all ages, assume that when a crime is committed against them by a parent, that they themselves are to blame. After all, as children we have no choice but to trust our parents. We are at their mercy and, being children, we assume that mercy will be granted.

When I was in law school, we used to joke about a lenient judge whose nickname was "Turn 'em Loose Bruce." My friend is like Turn 'em Loose. She let her mother walk when she should have sent her up the river. But how to change patterns of behavior now, when she's never confronted her mother before? Never confronted her, when at twelve she began to realize that the life she was living was not necessarily her own. That the notes she and friends passed to each other in class were removed from her notebook and read, as were letters she received from friends from summer camp and notes from herself, the writing in her diary that helped her know what she was thinking. Before thoughts were barely her own they were claimed by her mother. No wonder she confused the robber and the robbed.

To this day she bears the guilt rather than bearing the thought of her mother as untrustworthy. At least when Turn 'em Loose Bruce lets them walk, he doesn't take on the mantle of the alleged crime. He doesn't confuse himself with the person appearing before him at the bench. No. When he turns 'em loose, he slips out of his robe and goes home for a nice dinner with friends and family. Maybe takes in a show. He lives his life.

My friend isn't as fortunate. She freed her mother and imprisoned herself.

Recent anti-abortionist challenges to *Roe v. Wade*, the 1973 Supreme Court decision that made abortion legal, contest whether a right to privacy is guaranteed by the Bill of Rights. In 1965, in *Griswold v. Connecticut*, the case that would become the cornerstone of *Roe*, Justice William O. Douglas asserted that it was guaranteed. That case reversed the convictions of the executive and medical directors of the Planned Parenthood League of Connecticut, who had violated Connecticut statutes making it a crime to use or aid and abet another's use of "any drug, medicinal article or instrument" for birth control purposes. Douglas viewed such statutes as gross intrusions by the state into the private lives of its citizens, and asked, "Would we allow the police to search the sacred precincts of marital bedrooms for telltale signs of the use of contraceptives?" The right to privacy, he asserted, was even "older than the Bill of Rights." Our founding fathers understood that without it we could not become a civilized society.

It is no accident that those who drafted the Bill of Rights are referred to as "founding fathers." Their concerns about the role of the State in the individual lives of citizens were based on notions of good parenting. The State, after all, is a form of institutional parent, and as with parents, what must be guarded against is the abuse of power by those stronger than those they are dutybound to protect. They knew that the right to privacy, what Justice Louis D. Brandeis would refer to as the "right to be let alone," is the foundation of trust. And they understood that if citizens were always watching their backs, they could not go about the essential business of forging ahead to found a nation. Similarly, in our own homes, with our own families, if we are always watching our backs, we are not free to forge ahead to become ourselves.

Regardless of the outcome, if the court addresses this issue again, the fact that it is being debated is a reminder that a right to privacy is more than a nicety; it has been proclaimed a "fundamental" right.

I think many parents forget this. I have a friend who told me proudly, "Wow! Can my daughter ever write!" and then elaborated on how she had been reading her daughter's "secret" notebooks and come across a "rivetting short story." A recent biography of short story writer Shirley Jackson reveals that the young Jackson burned everything she ever wrote and suffered an incurable sense of betrayal upon discovering her grandmother reading the private notebooks she had filled with adolescent poetry. I think parents sometimes assume that such trespass is harmless. Not so. My friend whose mother read her diaries and letters has never learned to trust. She does not keep a journal, will not confide in friends. She carries her life bound to her back, as brittle and burdensome as a carapace.

She also lacks the judgment that comes with having experienced privacy. The judgment to know the difference between those things that should be revealed and those that should be guarded. Above all, she is incapable of trusting herself. Her instincts are suspect. All because the one person whose job it was to deliver her to a state of independence in which integrity could grow, bound her to herself, implying by her actions, "What's your business is my business."

In a letter to a friend who had betrayed him, Catullus wrote, "You led me into love as though all were safe for me."

In our eagerness to be loved, we imply our trustworthiness.

As we lead those we love to love, we vouchsafe the care of their hearts. The baggage with which they travel this tortuous route is trust, and there is no moving in, no coming home without it. The beloved does not expect, upon arrival, that the baggage will be stolen. It is the ultimate betrayal if it is.

How do we know when it's safe to unpack our bags and let our souls move in? In my own life, those I have loved and who have made it safe for me are people who mind their own business. I think of my husband, who never confuses my emotional and intellectual territory with his own. The fits and starts of my writing lie about the house on legal pads. It would never occur to him to read them unless I asked him to do so. He doesn't think twice about such restraint. I think about it all the time. It is my great luxury, this being entrusted with my own life.

I do not understand why my friend's mother worried that her daughter's secrets were somehow sinful and required her spying vigilance. Those fears must have been born of her own private demons. What I do understand is that secret lives are lives worth living. Our earliest secrets are steps to becoming individuals separate from our parents. Later, in adolescence, we can affect punk haircuts and slovenly dress, we can use outrage to set ourselves apart, but when we're very young, the only way to be independent from those on whom we're utterly dependent is to find a secret garden, where we can live secret lives. Secrets are our way of marking territory, of trying out and discovering who we are. If the boundaries we mark are invaded, so is the sense of self. And the right to self.

Even as an adult, I cherish the right to my secrets, most of which are as seemingly inconsequential as those of childhood. In fact, they are very similar to those of childhood. The silent observations and musings, those paths to ourselves.

I was fortunate that in being led into love, all *was* safe for me and I have tried to return the favor, to share with my daughter this gift from my husband, the certainty that intimacies shared and secrets unshared were equally secure. It's not easy, considering that curiosity is such a driving instinct. There have been times when there was no cooling my burning desire to know the news. To demand, "Okay, spill the beans." Or, "What do you mean, 'Nothing went on in school today'?" Or, "Where'd you go and what'd you do?" "Is it true your friend's mother is dating an Arab sheik?" Of course, sometimes I asked, I pried, I cajoled. Sometimes I was satisfied, and at other times I was disappointed. But there was also a thrill in the rude response that mothers abhor, "None of your business!" That response reminded me that she knew the difference between what was her business and what was mine. Those words reassured each of us of our own integrity.

It is the least we owe those we lead to love, those people who give us their hearts, and trust us with their lives.

On Mystery

....

It is reported that there is a forty-year-old woman, J. Z. Knight, who claims to be the "channel" for Ramtha, a 35,000-year-old man. That is, when she opens her mouth (for money from her New Age followers), his words come out. I know the feeling well. Especially at 6:30 on Monday mornings when the alarm goes off.

It was with the temperament of a 35,000-year-old curmudgeon that I, on assignment for a newspaper, approached my first psychic experience. "What do you want to do that for?"

My friend the feisty physicist reacted as though I had reported a decision to forsake my vows to a religious order. The order of reason. William James determined that thinkers are divided into two groups. The tough-minded and the tender-minded. My friend is tough-minded, with the exception of her reactions to Bach, trees, and the tricks of atoms.

"It's not a stand against weirdness," she assures me. "Physics is a lot stranger than anything psychics have come up with. The difference is that all the bizarre things in physics follow fairly logically from simple ideas." She is very taken with cause and effect. "The miracles of physics can repeat themselves over and over. A psychic might make a good guess, but it can't be repeated." "Look, it's an assignment. I'm just as cynical as the next guy," I assure her, as if this were a contest. "Then why waste your time?" "Curiosity," I tell her, rising to the occasion, "is never a waste of time."

Was I curious for the same reason that Columbus was, or that anthropologists, neurologists, and astronomers are? Because there is something about a horizon that makes you want to peek over the edge?

I call Forrester Church, a theologian respected for the fine tuning of his tough and tender thinking. "History tells us these people have always existed," I say and remind him of oracles, priests, and the possessed. He agrees. "There are far too many evidences of these special gifts in every age and every time to discount." And assures me that there is no doubt that "there are those who pierce the veil of reality more incisively than others." With this nod from history and theology, I set out upon my quest.

A veteran detective with the police department gives me the name of a woman who has been consulted successfully in his line of work. But when I call, Charles, a cordial young man who acts as her secretary, tells me that she's booked for a year. "I feel terrible turning so many people away. One of our clients is a psychiatrist and she tells me I shouldn't feel so bad. 'Just say no,' she says. But I still feel bad." I offer him the opportunity to assuage his guilt. "Perhaps you could answer a few questions?" He'd be delighted. "Are most of the clients men or women?" "Women. Men are too rigid in their thinking. But when their wives or girlfriends or whatever bring them, they come as sceptics and go bananas." "Go bananas?" "Yep. She tells them things about themselves and it scares them. She loses a lot of clients that way."

But the vacancies left by those beating a hasty retreat are filled from a long waiting list. "In one year we've received 8,750 calls from around the world. Paris. London. Geneva."

Some claim that this current clamor is the result of our living in troubled times. I disagree. All times are troubled times. According to Sir James Frazer, the belief in temporary inspiration and the gift of prophesy is universal and age-old. I would suggest that the desire to consort with spirits is less the sign of troubled times than of our eternal attraction to what is just beyond knowing.

Before hanging up, Charles gives me the name of a "highly respected" woman in the field and warns against charlatans. "Never go into one of those storefront fortune-telling parlors. They're dangerous. And never, under any circumstances, go to the Ansonia Hotel."

Avoiding both, I arrive at the approved address and am greeted by a freckled redhead who introduces herself as Mary. She could be a salesgirl in Ralph Lauren's Polo Shop. I had expected something a little bit, well, smokier. Gypsy hoops rather than pearl studs. Flowered skirts, not wool tweed. Full breasts and hips, not this wisp of a young woman. Her up-

turned nose lends her the air of an ingenue. She leads me into
the comfortable living room of her apartment. There are no
playing cards, no crystal ball, or incense fumes. A grandmother from Iowa could live here.

Before arriving, I had removed all traces of taste and personality. Removed my rings and worn the suit I had worn
when I practiced law—the kind women wear when they want
to be invisible. I had determined that if I was going to play,
I was going to play psychic hardball. She'd have to work for
her seventy-five-dollar fee and my conversion.

"Writer," she says, before we've taken our places on opposite sides of the room, she in a green velvet wing chair and
I on a matching couch. "Writer comes up all around you."
Was there an aura that she perceived the way the rest of us
witness physical manifestations? Or had she seen my byline?
You, I remind myself, have been trained in facts. It is fact,
not illusion, that leads to the truth.

Later my physicist friend is to assert, "Do you know what
a safe guess that was? Of the ten families on my street, I can
tell you there are at least eight people who feel they're meant
to be writers. If she had said the same thing to one of them,
they would have thought, 'She knows my deepest desire.' "

But how to explain her ability to report the intimate details
of the lives of my family members? And how to explain why,
at a certain moment, I determined to suspend disbelief and
turn myself over to experience? Perhaps if my background
had been in physics, I would not have gone for the psychic.
My physicist friend and I share a need to find the miraculous
in the mundane. I might argue the particulars. A forty-year-
old who takes her show on the road with a 35,000-year-old
man and earns millions as a result might try my capacity for
belief. And ending up at a cocktail party with a bunch of New

Age afficionadoes speaking tremulously of signs and auras and charts and past lives makes me feel as though I'm trapped in Bloomingdale's on Saturday. But I do believe that mystery exists and that some things are to be taken on faith rather than on proof.

"You know, it's not beyond the realm of possibility that the psychic might see things I do not," I tell the physicist. "This could end our friendship," she warns. "And furthermore, if you believe that, it's because that's what you want to believe." It *could* be that that's what I want to believe, but as I sit across from the putative seer, I dispense with wishing and watch with the caginess of reporter and attorney. It is true that I would be pleased to catch her up. It would make a better story. Before I arrived, the slant I would take was already in mind. This was to be a satirical article, poking fun at all the fuss over the occult.

She focuses her eyes, first on my own and then on the space between us. After ten minutes in the room, I begin to sense something in that space, something shimmering, like a mirage above asphalt on a hot summer day. This is where she seems to "pick things up." This is where she seems to "see" my husband before I have mentioned marital status. She says, "Well, this sounds funny, but I keep picking up . . . ," and she names a little-known historical figure. "That's who your husband is like." Later, when I return home and report this, my husband responds, "That's interesting. That's the third time today someone has said I remind them of him."

I have not yet said a word beyond the introduction, and yet she begins to speak of other members of my family. "When your father was in college, he seriously considered becoming a lawyer, which he did not." This is true. (It is also true, I grant you, that many men of my father's generation and breeding considered becoming lawyers.) She mentions that I am particularly fond of a four-year-old niece. Also true, and a bit rarer than male aspirations to the bar.

I find myself beginning mentally to applaud her efforts when they're on target and be disappointed when they're off. Suddenly I want her to be right because I long for the capacity of the human spirit to be boundless. I want to be amazed. But, no, there is no important person in my life named Peter, and I have not been to Morocco.

Soon after my story was published, I received a letter from a vice-president of an investment banking firm. She told me that the psychic had probably picked up her late husband, Peter, who had died two months before and had always been a "big talker." Many of their friends had reported seeing him. "And his favorite place on earth was Morocco." It seems he could have scrambled the psychic airwaves. Beware, you big talkers.

There had been no time to research my background between the time I called for the appointment and the moment I arrived on her doorstep. And even if there had been, she was telling me facts that had never been publicly reported. How she arrived at them remains a mystery.

"Not as mysterious as a tree," my friend responds. I don't tell her that's a sentiment she shares with the Druids. Nor do I argue the wonder of quarks, gluons, and black holes in space. She reminds me that physicist Frank Oppenheimer liked to say, "Science is the search for the ever-juicier mystery." I assert that all of life is a search for the ever-juicier mystery, and that wherever it's found, the least we can do is approach, without bias, and wonder. The least we can do is be amazed.

On Solitude

if I in my north room
dance naked, grotesquely
before my mirror
waving my shirt round my head
and singing softly to myself:
"I am lonely, lonely.
I was born to be lonely,
I am best so!"

Who shall say I am not
the happy genius of my household?

WILLIAM CARLOS WILLIAMS

....

When I tell my friend who is walking toward her guest house, arms full of Pratesi sheets, that I don't allow summer house-guests, she stops and addresses me with a mixture of incredulity and disapproval. "But what do you say when a cousin calls from California and asks to come East to spend a few days?" I shrug. She grows more agitated. "What about your best friend who happens to be city-bound in August? Not even a weekend? You wouldn't even offer her an over-night?"

"Nope."

I am more direct now than I was when I first decided to change our summer life-style. Then, my responses were as weighted with guilt as Goethe's letters to abandoned friends back in the court of Weimar—those not invited along when under an assumed name he caught a night mail coach bound for Italy and solitude.

"I am so happy that you have taken my disappearance as well as I hoped you would," he wrote, probably knowing full well that they considered his actions selfish and bohemian. "Please make my peace with any heart that may have been offended at it. I did not mean to upset anyone and I cannot yet say anything to justify myself. God forbid that the motives which led to my decision should ever hurt the feelings of a friend."

God forbid. How to justify to friends a desire to spend August solely in the company of family? It takes time for words to rendezvous with resonance of the heart. Time and age for action to catch up with instinct. This seems especially true when to answer the call of instinct would take us from the table of convention. When we are told that the call is for us, it's hard to ask gracefully, "May I be excused?"

The decision to boycott houseguests was not a sudden one. It followed a slow, unplanned ebb into solitude. It was a preference that grew as I left my frenzied twenties and thirties, a time of acquiring friends and approval. It was not that we didn't enjoy the camaraderie of summer cocktail parties, the chance to catch up with friends whose busy city lives had kept us apart, to engage in that particular kind of vacation conversation that moves easily from thought provoking philosophizing to idle gossip. It was not a conscious decision to participate less. We simply allowed the sea to take hold.

A six P.M. summer sky turns water to gold and then to hues of rose and purple. Other skippers furl sail, head home, don red trousers and hoist gin and tonics. We were alone out here, left to ourselves and each other. Without plans, subterfuge, or stealth we had sailed into the bliss of solitude. We may not have known it yet, but we were developing a taste for solitary confinement—the kind that frees the soul.

However, seclusion excludes. Your retreating back will be pelleted by buckshots of accusations. "You seem to have dropped out of our lives." The hurt voice on the other end of the phone belongs to the doyenne of our summer community's social life. She informs me that it is unseemly to flaunt a persistent preference for privacy, for the company of one's spouse and child above all others. I stare at my feet, the toes begin to turn inward. I have automatically assumed the posture of a two-year-old who has been caught being herself. In my forties, more and more I am caught being myself.

I would make amends. I would fashion the moral equivalent of Goethe's letters. I'd give a cocktail party. I invite my caller immediately. She accepts with pleasure and adds, "You know I love you, darling, otherwise I wouldn't tell you these things."

I list my guests on paper and my sins in my mind. Who did I think I was, giving myself over to Henry James and Jane Austen and Chekhov, and lovemaking and long naps after lunch? What had I done to deserve silence and daydreams? I would confess self-indulgence and redeem the sated self. I ordered Scotch. (On our island, real men still drink Scotch. If they've ever heard of a spritzer, they probably think it's something their wives use in the garden or on their hair.) I dreaded the event. When it occurred, I had a good time. We like our friends.

And yet, was the pleasure of their company a match for the enchantment of an unscheduled evening, following an unplanned day? If the breezes blew from the right direction, we might sail to the neighboring island of my childhood and return with baskets full of the bounty of the sea and my parents' garden. Once home, there is no need to take off the favorite old salt encrusted sweater. Pots are set to boil, a bit of water for the fresh corn, wine for the mussels. One hand stirs while the other holds a book and Jane Austen's garden paths take on the perfumes of barnacle and brine.

When it is time for attention to turn exclusively to family, there's no need to show Mr. Darcy to the door, I just close the book and we're alone. If there are the two or three of us at dinner, conversation is a matter of choice, not form. If the spirit moves us, we can just stare out silently at the fog as it tucks us in for the night. We toast each other in all the languages we can muster (two and a half). And reach across the table for a hand, a ritual. A way of saying, I love you. Thank you for this moment. It would not happen with guests present because the most important work of a hostess is to make the invited feel included, and the deep familial secrets of love are by nature exclusive.

As darkness falls, we light a fire to catch and dry the evening dampness persistently pushing its way beneath our doorstep. We listen for the whippoorwill. If we're lucky that's our only call. We step out on the deck to bid reluctant farewells to day and light. Fog falls on our eyelashes and settles there. We listen for the bell buoy that has sung us to sleep for all the years of our lives together. Far across the water, where bay meets open sea, comes the haunting sound of the foghorn that filled us with loneliness as we lay in the separate beds of our childhoods. These are the sounds and memories that bind families and give them a sense of place. Would they be heard above the happy chatter shared with visiting friends?

We have determined that August is the time for life to have its way with us. Given our druthers, each day would be lived in response to wind and tide rather than schedule and engagement. This cannot be done when there are ferries to be met and meals to be planned. You can't live off the whims of blueberry bushes, wild sorrel, and whatever happens to be in the lobster pot when there are expectant mouths about the table. You can't bask in silence when ears await the news of your life. Our friends deserve better than the passivity we pursue. They deserve our attention—and they've got it. But not for these thirty-one days. Perhaps before departing for this summer's retreat, I'll leave a recording of that plaintive "golden oldie" on my answering machine: "See you in September, or lose you to a summer love. . . ."

And lose them I might, to all those kind people with generous hearts and guest houses. But what I have gained is the peace that comes from moving on the wind's way and sharing days with birds, berries that ripen in the sun, deer that walk in the forests, and a husband and daughter whose lives are as overextended, overscheduled, and remote as all Manhattan lives the remaining eleven months of the year. These thirty-one days are for silences and the rhythms of sea and heart. Rhythms that can't be heard above the spatter of eggs being fried for hungry houseguests.

On Passion

....

It's usually safer to listen to external murmurs than to those
of our own hearts. If it's safety we want.

Passion's path is perilous. It takes us to silent rooms where
there's nothing to do but stare at empty canvases or computer
screens or blank sheets of paper. Passion asks, "Now what?"
And expects an answer. It inflicts the terrible loneliness of
feeling deeply and hearing no responding, "Me too," or
"That's interesting," or "Good idea!" Sometimes it's years
between one "Good idea!" and another. It's less lonely to

undertake what the world expects of us than what we expect of ourselves. Easier to follow movements hither and yon, getting caught up in their momentum rather than our own.

Some of us who followed the women's movement thought that we could dissipate despair from women's lives by storming the male barricades. We determined that that was the path to deliverance, the way to dispell a sense of insignificance. What we failed to realize, is that all human beings, male and female, feel insignificant. And why shouldn't we, when we compare ourselves to trees and stars and Aristotle? But that doesn't make it so. Significance comes from becoming who we were meant to be, by following the path that passion leads. We removed some of the obstacles in that path, but we also lost track of the heart of the matter.

In the early days of that movement there were masses of women looking at their feet and muttering, "I'm just a mother," to the inevitable question of that period: "And what do you *do?*" "To do" meant to be a member of one of those professions that leant power to men. Few of us under the age of forty had the self-awareness and security to know that who we were and how we lived our lives and fought our fights could not be dictated by others, even if those others were our allies.

Unfortunately, the movement gave birth to a generation that has failed to learn this. These archetypes of the eighties are as bland and lifeless as the pastel protagonists on the pages of fifties first grade primers. Who are they?

He, secure in his profession at thirty-five, takes a wife who is equally secure, although still working her way to the top. For tax reasons and for investment, they purchase a co-op or condominium.

By the time she's thirty-five, she becomes pregnant. Amniocentesis lets the parents know that the baby suffers no genetic defects and is a boy.

A room is prepared. Educational toys, stimulating mobiles, a state-of-the-art stroller. The prospective parents attend Lamaze classes together and discuss "parenting" with the heavy sententiousness of Talmudic scholars. They fill their library with books and videotapes on the subject. They, unlike their parents before them, are going to do it "right."

Once the baby is born, it becomes the focus of their attentions, replacing previous preoccupations with electronics and second homes. Slowly their lives begin to resemble those they damned their parents for living. Lives lived "through" the children. Something eludes them—although profession, child, and material gain have been achieved.

It's a frightening odyssey to go in search of what's missing and to change our lives. It feels safer and less taxing to live blandly rather than boldly, to live by what, rather than who we are. But it turns out that unless it is our calling, unless our work is fueled by passion, becoming a member of an acceptable profession, a lawyer or a doctor, for instance, does not necessarily bestow an identity. It does not automatically qualify us as people to be taken seriously, as grown-ups in a grown-up world. Unfortunately, graduate degrees and titles alone do not impart substance.

We didn't know this at a time when few of us had either. But, as we began to achieve them, we also began to speak with disdain of the women we left "behind." We saw them as "child wives," "child mothers," somehow less adult than ourselves. How foolish and how fatuous we were. There are cowards and undeveloped people in all professions, and just as many wise and mature wives and mothers as there are wise and mature physicians, attorneys, poets. It has taken time to learn that our real work is not necessarily to survive graduate school and to obtain an office with a view, but rather to hunt down our passions, our callings, and to dare to let them lead us where they may.

I believe that each of us has a calling. But to hear the call and to respond to it takes nerves of steel. How else will we dare have faith in our minds and hearts, and in their inclinations?

When I began practicing law with a highly respected Manhattan law firm, the eight law school graduates who started with me formed a particularly attractive, lively, and diverse group. By the end of our fifth month together, six of the young men were wearing red suspenders exactly like those worn by one of the senior partners. Three began to smoke his brand of cigars, and all adopted his cautious, tight-lipped manner. They were, in other words, every bit as submissive as that old-fashioned wife the movement sought to deliver. They attached their identity to his, as eagerly and willingly as she did to a stronger man. They surrendered themselves.

After a year and a half in practice, I determined that being a lawyer was not how I wanted to live my life. That, in spite of all the training, the time, the expense, and the investment, I was going to leave the law in order to write. When I announced my decision to the partners, many responded with a wistful, "I wish I could do that."

I think a life of wishes, once we are adult, is no life at all. It is one thing, as children, when we are powerless, to turn to stars and wishbones and candles on a cake to make our dreams come true. But as adults, we need none of that. We can take charge of our dreams—if we dare.

There were many two A.M.'s when I didn't think I would dare. The realization that I must quit the law in order to be the person I am was accompanied by great anxiety. What made me think I had the right? Wouldn't it be cheating in some way? What if I failed? Was one entitled to take a leap for joy when joy was not guaranteed? And what of the partners who had hired me in good faith, had held their collective breaths because I was seen, back then in 1979, as a terrible risk? I was a woman with other commitments—a woman with a family. They were right, I was not a good investment, but not for the reasons they feared. I was a bad risk because the law did not have my heart and soul. I did not want to become just like the man with the red suspenders and the big cigar.

And what of the women's movement? Wasn't I failing it, and thus weakening the cause? Other women accused me of this. "How can you turn your back on all that?" they asked. "All that" being what they saw as a fearless future: a guaranteed income, possible power, and independence.

It turns out that "all that" isn't everything. And knowing what I know now, even if I were not supported financially, I would turn my back on "all that." I would live simply and support my habit with a rural postal route, a quiet job with time for contemplation.

But, I didn't know that in the days before I had begun to pursue a career in what was then regarded as a man's world. I didn't know that on the day back then as I sat in the lobby of the Harvard Club waiting to meet a friend and enviously watching the men enter with preoccupied expressions, heavy briefcases, and shiny wing-tip shoes. Now *those* are real grown-ups, I thought, and I wanted to be part of what I perceived to be their purposefulness. Their seriousness. Yes, their self-satisfaction.

The first time I went to the Harvard Club after I had quit the law, I looked at those men and became aware that each of us regarded the other as the grown-up, and ourselves as the imposter.

The myth of the grown-up. People are mythmakers, so there will always be fictions to influence what we do with our lives. When the fictions no longer serve us, when they are revealed as fallible rather than ideal, we replace them with other dreams. Unfortunately, the current replacements are too small and mean to support a sense of the heroic. They will turn on us, just as the myths of the fifties turned on the women who tried to live them—to be the mom in the kitchen, the source of apple pies, laps and hugs, familial happiness and sexual pyrotechnics. This ideal, propagated by men, a conspiracy of aunts, mothers, grandmothers, and women's magazines, imprisoned them. Similarly today, the "new happiness," affluence, provided by a professional husband-and-wife team, has limited rather than liberated lives. Once we determine to support myth against reason and humanity, once we surrender independent decision-making, and cease listening to ourselves, we become subservient, less human.

If we dare become what passion bids us to become, it is possible that we might return to the world a sense of the heroic. At the very least we'll bring it life in the form of our poetry, painting, dance, and thoughtful humanity. Passion is not a selfish thing because it is capable of awakening the passion of others.

As far as we know, we only pass through this life once. At least the evidence to the contrary isn't strong enough to bank on a second act. And so we might as well do it on extended wings. We might as well dare to soar and sing and dance as live defensively. We might as well arm ourselves with courage and hunt down our passions, and once we've found them, cling to them as a lioness clings to her cubs—with a tender but ferocious grip.

LOOKING
BACK

"Frogs Eat Butterflies.
Snakes Eat Frogs.
Hogs Eat Snakes.
Men Eat Hogs"

WALLACE STEVENS

....

Girls, they say, are afraid of bugs, and so my husband kills the spider.

"Not with a Kleenex!" I warn him. "Use a box. With Kleenex you'll feel the crunch."

Of course roaches are worse. With a roach, no matter how large the weapon, you will hear the carapace collapse. You will feel the slow reluctant give. I leave the room before contact.

"I ain't afraid of no bug!" I protested at ten, imitating the local lingo and longing for the company of boys. I yearned for their acceptance, for entry into their muddy games, their fits and starts, giggles, kicking, rolling, hitting. Their life force. Their freedom. They offered escape from tea parties for dolls. From a dusty, still, indoor life. Relief for legs and arms that felt like elastic bands stretched to the snapping point. I longed to be propelled into their adventures, expeditions to haunted houses, overnights, and campfires.

"Oh, yeah?" said Sean with his hands behind his back. "If you like bugs so much, how about this one." His fingers were suddenly beneath my nose. He dangled the daddy longlegs before me as if it were a Christmas ornament. I smiled. My feet went cold. I stood my ground. He pulled off the legs one by one.

Such malice was fueled by his primitive sense of truth: Girls are afraid of bugs and boys are afraid of girls.

Thus the threshold guardians of the male barricades were in place: daddy longlegs, centipedes, beetles, and things un-named squirming beneath logs.

Reptiles were less effective tools of terror, even though we were warned that playing with toads would give us warts. David was proof of that: A collector of toads, he had brown, lumpy hands to show for it. I was willing to risk such a fate in order to hold a toad or salamander or frog.

I mastered the technique of taking them alive. Lie flat. Breathe as you imagine the grass breathes. Move as you imagine the earth moves. You've got all day. You've got all of childhood to make your way, flat on your belly to the edge of the pond, to a lily pad that supports a sleeping frog. The glistening green of ponds and frogs urges you on.

There have been few victories in my life as triumphant as the hand that closes, not on itself, but on the throbbing surprise of a frog. We both open our eyes at the same time, stare, and breathe hard. We've each made a plunge for life, and this time I'm the winner. Belly down and breathless, staring into bulging eyes.

As I was on the edge of ponds, so the life of boys was on the edge of danger. Their talk was of copperheads, bears, and ominous things lurking in swamp and forest. They were attracted to these dark depths, to that which was beyond the sight of girls. If they held us in fear, they held us at bay.

We waited in the sunlight. We stood waiting to be scared. Shrieking before there was reason to shriek. Living in fear of the sudden appearance of something with many legs fighting for its life. Such a wild display quickened the heart and made one run for one's life. Or away from it.

Sense of Place

....

I am uncertain whether it is the land or the people inhabiting the land that gives one a sense of place. If you read *Far Away and Long Ago,* W. H. Hudson's moving autobiography of his boyhood in Argentina, you are quite certain it is the land. That the foundation for a sense of place is animism, a belief, not uncommon among children, that the earth and all that grows therein possess a soul, a spirit similar to one's own. Hudson's book is less biography than the story of mutual love shared with the trees, flowers, and birds of the pampas.

It may be the land that makes the primal claim, when a child, locked in early muteness, has a natural affinity for the silent lives of trees and terrain. But it is the people that bring drama to a place. And it is drama that gives rise to the storytelling of later years. Stories that make it possible for the mind to return to a place long since departed.

When my sister and I reminisce, those of whom we speak could be characters created by Welty, Faulkner, or Hardy. Many of the children with whom we shared overheated classrooms came to school straight from the barnyard and morning chores. When it was "rest time," and Mrs. Murdoch played the piano and sang the sad song of Bobby Shaftoe going to sea, those weary laborers fell into deep sleep. Resting their heads on arms held in a fold by hands creased with brown.

We sometimes speak of the man in the hollow, who was a collector and would swap his things for your things. His refrigerator door for your car fender. Four worn tires for a picture frame buffed with gilt. Only weeds and rust claimed a plow that, in winter, protruded from snow like the rib cage of a fallen animal. And nobody ever had a swap for the claw-footed bathtub that rested among choke weed and Queen Anne's lace.

Unlike Hudson's, these memories comprise a one-sided love affair. If you, a stranger, were to pass through and ask the swapper if he remembers us, chances are he'd scratch his chin, do you the courtesy of repeating our names and feigning thought. He would appear to search the horizon the way one might investigate a row of books in a library stack. "Nope, can't say that I do," he'd say, and kick some gravel with his worn boot to dismiss you.

If you entered the schoolyard, a pasture where cows no

longer graze, if you stopped at the swing set or baseball diamond, and asked after us, you might get a giggle and a quick shake of the head before losing your witness to a game of tag.

It's as if we were never there.

Sense of place is bolstered by a cruel, unrequited love. It takes hold insidiously as scents, scenes, and the corners of rooms become objects of eternal passion. When does the place where you rest your head become a matter for the heart to contend with? And how does the place you claim turn around and claim you?

"Former lives," a friend explains, and quickly adds, "Look, I'm not weird or from California or anything, I'm a very sensible down-to-earth person." But she thinks in a former life she lived near London's Covent Garden. She says it's the only way to explain her sense of peace when she's there as compared to the displacement she felt as a child. "I never felt at home where I lived in upstate New York. I remember, when I was eight years old, sitting on the back steps and thinking, 'I don't belong here.' "

I remember when I was eight years old, sitting beneath the eaves of my room and thinking, I do belong here. I belonged, not only in that room, but to the hills, pastures and the old apple tree outside my window. A tree with peeling bark and gnarled limbs that managed annual rejuvenations, bursts of energy each spring and fall bringing sweet and spicy perfumes. Scents set in a young girl's heart.

Scents that gave one a sense of place.

Beyond the tree, past the barn and pasture, set on the rise of a distant hill was China. If I had read Blake, I could just as easily have thought it was Jerusalem. Years later, when riding our horses there for picnics and the view, I would laugh at my earlier perspective. But it is that perspective that remains, somehow encompassing the mystery of what it means to be home.

When we left, twenty-four years ago, slamming the car doors, and driving away through the twilight, we were uncertain whether to close our eyes to deny departure or to stare, to cling with vision as a young child outside a schoolyard might hold fast to a mother's skirts. The smell of hay and cows and barnyards grew heavy in the damp as cooling night fell like a curtain coming down. We would never again be on the other side. From then on we were audience.

The difference between being at home and not is that, if you are not, you are always the outsider looking in: sometimes amused and entertained by what you see, but always displaced and alone, and a bit uncomfortable in your seat, even if you're surrounded by others sharing the darkened theater. It's brighter and warmer up there on the stage where people belong to each other and the scenery.

Eudora Welty is at home in Jackson. William Faulkner was at home in Oxford. Although their gifts suggest that they would have written wherever they had been born and raised, I doubt their writings would shine with that peculiar and passionate energy had the authors not been born to places responsive to their spirits.

This bonding is described in Welty's essay, "Some Notes on River Country." "A place that ever was lived in is like a fire that never goes out. It flares up, it smolders for a time, it is fanned or smothered by circumstance, but its being is intact, forever fluttering within it, the result of some original ignition."

No one is left to tell you, should you wander into the valley of my home, that there was an ignition, a flame. But then,

nobody ever saw it light. That happens in the intimate encounter of a young heart with a particular arch of a hill, or
evening smells in rain or the sound of snow plows scraping a
country road at two A.M. It is just like falling in love. If you
try to remember how it happened, you may speak of being
captivated by a graceful curve of hip, the melody of a voice,
or the slant of eye. You will point to landmarks of the heart's
path, but you'll be unable to re-create the journey.

Good Behavior

Our guardians were skinny spinsters and sad-eyed widows. Lacking experience and clinging to breeding, they sought refuge as housemothers in our girls' boarding school. What did they teach of being women? To apologize. To beg your pardon for our sorrow, our clumsiness. To be vigilant and ruthlessly in control of libido. Sweetness was a virtue, confused with a value. This was no place for the loudmouth, the troublemaker, rebels with and without causes. Our guardians made life very difficult for them. They were grounded. Weekend privileges denied. The rare walk into town forbidden.

I was lucky. I heeded their lessons well, behaved myself, and suffered from acne. Good behavior made the ladies look upon me favorably, and the acne got me a pass, every Friday afternoon, to walk, unescorted, through town, out the other side, over a bridge to the dermatologist's office. Freedom! Out into a world in which children walked home from school. Mothers drove by in station wagons. Old people strolled, and come spring, all of them dropped to their knees in well-groomed flower beds.

My freedom was not, of course, as complete as theirs, the old people, the mothers, the children. The guardians fell in step behind me in the form of guilt, always at my heels prepared to nip and drag me back to the confines of my conscience should I stray from the annointed path of boarding school morals and manners.

If you were to ask our parents or the guardians themselves for what purpose were we turned over to their care, "for a fine education" would have been the unanimous response. But I have begun to wonder. Wonder as I flip through the alumni bulletin and learn how we are spending our lives. My old friends speak of house guests and new homes. Of travels to foreign ports.

I have lost contact with former classmates, but recently met one of us in adult flesh. An editor I was working with turned out to be an old friend who had been in the class ahead of mine. When, over lunch, I asked her what she thought of our previous existence, she looked away and winced. "Let's not talk about it," she said, and brought us back instantly to the matter at hand, our adulthood. Our work.

Did they expect us to work? I think not. I think that, whether they knew it or not, the teachers expected our lots to be that of other graduates, the well-groomed, gracious, and intelligent wives of high-powered men. From 1961 until my senior year in 1964, what I learned about more than history or math or science was how to behave. We were all learning how to behave.

We were certainly not learning how to think, except at the hands of a few teachers who were so eccentrically individual that the words out of their mouths jarred and troubled. It was impossible to follow the twists and turns of their intellects if we remained in the familiar lockstep.

Our lessons in how to be good began first thing in the morning as we marched to chapel. Just outside the door to forgiveness and hope, stood a senior, the head of the dress committee, with a pad and pencil in her hand and an eye trained to take in an offending hem, untied shoelace, painted nail, bit of jewelery that was "out of uniform." Neatness, being "in uniform" was like sweetness, an important human value. I don't recall what happened if you were "out of uniform," but I do know that none of us wanted our names written on that pad.

Last year, that head of the dress committee showed up with a daughter in my own daughter's school. When she recognized me and approached, I was surprised by a sense of foreboding. I was no longer adult, I was somehow scruffy and inadequate. She, of course, was neat as a pin. She asked me to call. She said we ought to get together. Never.

The world that drifted to girls' boarding schools in those days was not the world we would enter, but we feared it might be the world to which we would return in the end. The widows came because they had no other work, and being a housemother would provide food and shelter. Albeit institutionalized food and shelter. We were so accustomed to the lack of individuality and the absence of the primacy of desire, that it did not strike us as strange that free, consenting adults would choose to eat creamed chicken and tapioca every week and sleep on the same lumpy mattresses that had held the erotic dreams of past lonely women. We assumed that these women, like ourselves, had no choices. We sensed that we were victims together, bound by a lack of joy and an ignorance of our own power.

Some of the spinsters came because here they could prevail. They could frighten and reduce us to tears with their rage and bitterness. They could leave the world they had disappointed and that had disappointed them and reign triumphant within these confining walls. Remaining single was not, in those days, a choice. It was a curse. This was not like the Benedictine nunneries of the Middle Ages, which women of high birth entered in order to educate and free themselves of the constraints of marriage. This was the last resort, becoming the guardians of young girls they did not wish well. Each morning they checked our rooms for cleanliness. Each night for lights out. And in between for general good character. That is, a smile and sweet demeanor.

How could we not begin to think like them? They were the women with whom we spent the most time, our sleeping as well as waking hours. They sat dourly at the head of the table and oversaw our table manners. I don't remember any of them discussing the news. The outside world, for all intents and purposes, did not exist. We sat in a pine-paneled dining room, beneath imposing portraits of past, grim headmistresses. The food served was so bland that there was no danger of arousing our palates.

How different would our lives have been if in one of those portraits, a woman had had a gleam in her eye? Or posed with a dog or child or husband? What if there was a promise of fun? Of love? Of something grander than ourselves and the women with whom we lived in gloomy monotony and bitter resignation?

Recently, I met a man from Boston who was telling me about his men's club, a self-selective group of twenty-five who gather monthly in tuxedoes to dine and share "intellectual discourse." If, after a prospective newcomer is brought to one of these dinners, he follows the evening with a phone call rather than a thank you note, "He is not invited back." My new acquaintance expressed dismay: "You'd be surprised by how many don't know you're supposed to write a thank you note, not make a phone call."

We, graduates of my school, would never have failed this test. Nor would our husbands, because we would know to remind them. Thank goodness for that. We had learned to be supplicant and grateful, in form, if not in fact. We graduated with a comforting sense of moral superiority. A morality based on an allegiance to niceties. We did not confuse morals with niceties, there was no confusion whatsoever. A good person observed them. A bad person did not.

We were not daring enough in our thinking to ask, "Is Miss so-and-so a good person because she knows what to do with a dessert spoon and fork and one piece of cake?" Absolutely not. It was all part of the package. Community service and the proper use of utensils fell into the same bag of tricks into which a respectable person could reach.

We went forth into the world believing that we knew what really mattered. Now I wonder if this was defensive teaching, if we were taught that we knew best because the terrible secret was that, due to inbreeding, the aristocracy was losing brain power. Perhaps it was not until I saw the full and blooming range of my daughter's secondary school education that I knew the limits of my own. My daughter's teachers held her to task daily: Oh, that's what you think, do you? Why is that? What makes you think so? Can you support that with the books you've read? The paintings you've seen? Your knowledge of history?

No one expects that her life is to be spent at the head of a formally-dressed dinner table, wooing her husband's clients with her grace and charm.

Do we have the growth of feminism to thank for this? Yes, to the extent that feminism acknowledges women's potential. But when feminism moralizes that a woman is not "good" unless she's professional, its lessons are as meaningless as ours, that goodness could be measured in sweetness, with pickle forks. But the true thrust of feminism made it possible to take the minds of young girls seriously. It then made it a moral obligation. A teacher did not have to be eccentric to demand intellectual integrity. It became her job. Where our teachers often seemed to be vamping till ready, my daughter's teachers were engaged. After all, their charges were to become serious citizens of the world, not its decoration.

No one would argue that our teachers considered it unimportant to be educated. It just wasn't terribly important to know about cells and atoms and the joints of frogs. One brave soul considered it essential that we learn about Central America and the Far East. Attending his class was like attending the circus. Entertaining, but we knew it didn't have anything to do with real life.

The most memorable learning experience that came from those years, was the introduction to music. Musicians tend to operate outside the norm of any given time and place, and so our music teacher, complete with an exotic name of several syllables and ending in *o*, would appear, as if out of nowhere, every Wednesday afternoon to teach another movement of Mozart's *Requiem*. There would be no accompaniment. She would raise her arms, and on the downbeat we were expected to sight-read. Miraculously, it worked. Alto, soprano, and those in-between came forth in harmony. Week in, week out, we worked to know those notes as though we had written them ourselves. And then we were rewarded with the gift of an accompanying piano, and finally, the entire Boston Symphony.

Yes, music transcended everyone's expectations of what our lives were supposed to become. It was the one incident in which joy was the end in itself.

ABOUT THE AUTHOR

BARBARA LAZEAR ASCHER practiced law
for two years before becoming a writer
full time. She has published one book,
Playing After Dark, and her essays have
appeared in several anthologies, *The New
York Times, The Yale Review,* and other
publications. She lives with her family in
New York.